I0144920

Under the Staircase

Hearing God's Voice in the Darkness

By Darla Colinet

Copyright © 2016 by Darla Colinet

All rights reserved. This book or any portion thereof may not be reproduced or used in any manner whatsoever without the express written permission of the publisher except for the use of brief quotations in a book review.

Printed in the United States of America
First Printing, 2013

Cover design by Jennifer Top
Darla's
ISBN-10:0-9885088-2-6
ISBN-13:978-0-9885088-2-8

~This book is dedicated to Zafarrah, Louise, Loyce, LeRoy, Karen, and Buddy—all the Angel moms and dads who came beside me when I was heartbroken. Your love and encouragement were the beacons of faith and hope in my life. I could never find the right words to thank you enough.

Disclaimer: This work is a memoir. These are my memories, my perspective, and my story. It reflects my present recollection of my experiences over a period of years. To protect the privacy of others, certain names, locations, and identifying characteristics have been changed, and certain individuals are composites. Every effort was made to corroborate memory with fact but all human stories are subject to errors of omission, fact, or interpretation. Dialogue and events have been recreated from memory, and, in some cases, have been compressed to convey the substance of what was said or what occurred. I wrote this memoir with the intent to shine a light of hope to help others in similar dark places of their lives. No harm was ever intended.

"Once I began to read this insightful and heart wrenching memoir, I could not put it down..."

-Kate A. Johnson, MA, M.Div., LMHC, Executive Director of the Christian Coalition Against Domestic Abuse and Living in Freedom and Empowerment Ministry.

"*Under the Staircase* is a book of faith, bravery, and healing. At times it's reminiscent of Jeannette Walls's bestselling The Glass Castle..."

-Judge, Writer's Digest 21st Annual Self-Published Book Awards

"This compelling story reveals a journey with God in which pain and losses were experienced in various forms. Moments of doubt in the darkest hours exposed God's faithfulness to guide and direct as he rescued her out of the pit to restoration."

-Paula Silva, FOCUS Ministries Inc.

" *Under the Staircase* is a powerful real life story that brings a persevering and faithful God into clearer view in the midst of life's pain. Through her captivating journey Darla candidly shares how her own heart found all that it was looking for as God brought beauty out of the ashes and a treasured daughter from death to life."

-Rose Pauly, Pastor and Founder of Tenacious Love Ministries

Chapter 1

"History . . . is a nightmare from which I am trying to awake."
—Philip Roth

I entered the courtroom alone to face Mark, the husband who had abused me and my boys for years. I was sworn in and took a seat at the witness stand. All my fears about Mark taking the boys away from me punched me in the face.

My value in life existed in being a mother. My sons were the very reasons I lived, and now the legal system's rules left Mark in control. I couldn't run or hide. I had to protect the hearts of my sons no matter what it cost me. I had only one choice—to relinquish my custody. It was the only way to save my son's hearts and self-worth from being torn apart up on the witness stand. I asked the judge to remove the boys from the courtroom. Once they were gone, I announced my decision to surrender custody. Mark sneered in triumph. My heart disintegrated the minute the pen in my trembling hand inked my signature on the custody papers. I had to let them go to protect them. There was no other way out this time. I fled the courtroom and scrambled to find my car. Once inside, the blackness of my despair screamed my name. "Darla, you've failed again. You always do. Come down here and stop feeling your pain. Just disappear. No one will notice you're gone. They never do. What's the use of going on? Your boys are Mark's now and they will hate you for leaving them."

My mind flashed over the dozens of times I felt helpless to protect the boys from being hurt and abused. I should have killed Mark years ago to stop him. Mark was right. I was a horrible mother because I didn't protect them. I didn't deserve to care for my sons. Being their mom was the reason for my every breath. I'd failed; I'd been defeated. There was no reason to live.

Blackness overtook my mind until I saw a flicker in the dark. With all my remaining strength I cried out, "God, I've known and loved you as far back as my memory goes. How did I get to this point in my life? Please show me the road you have for me or I'm done." I wept and drifted into a soft, safe place of inconceivable peace. The story of my life began to unfold before me like a motion picture.

Chapter 2

"As individuals, we are shaped by story from the time of
birth; we are formed by what we are told by our parents,
our teachers, our intimates."
—Helen Dunmore

Snapshots of my life zoomed in and out, and I squeezed my head to make them focus. They settled on Daddy. He moved our family from California to Tehran, Iran in 1965. I was eight months old and my adopted brother Conner was two. A woman named Zafarrah helped Mom take care of us and the house when Daddy, who fixed airplanes for the Air Force, worked away from home. There were also large men who went everywhere with us. With age, I learned they were bodyguards assigned to our family to protect us from being kidnapped. We lived in a two-story brick house with bars on the doors and windows. Razor and electric wire crowned the fifteen-foot-high brick walls surrounding our backyard. This fortress was home and became a part of our normal life.

Daddy worked for weeks at a time and left us in the care of Zafarrah and Mom. I recall the aroma of scrambled eggs the moment my eyes opened in the morning when Daddy was home. He would laugh and play dolls with me, and we would finish our day with me atop of his shoes, whirling around the room to the sound of Jesus music. Daddy continually sang songs of love, joy, salvation, and flying away to heaven while he clapped his hands and chuckled. He sang one song when he was sad, "One day at a time, sweet Jesus, that's all I'm asking of you." This usually happened when Mom was in her far away place, staring out the window.

Sometimes Daddy took me to work with him. We started at the crack of dawn with a crazy, roofless jeep ride that followed no traffic rules or markers. We zoomed through narrow, crooked streets teeming with people, carts, and animals. An orchestra of horns, bells, and shouts accompanied by spastic hand motions gave me the giggles. Once we checked in at the airport security gate, Daddy drove to the back of an enormous gray cargo plane. We crept up the ramp inside the large metal bird, shrinking me to bug size. He locked the jeep in place and escorted me to the cockpit to start my copilot duties. He placed the man-sized head phones over my little girl ears and let me flip switches, push buttons, and turn knobs to start the engines. We taxied the plane along the runway to a hangar for repairs. To steer this big beast, to be Daddy's little girl for this short time, somehow made up for all the weeks and months he was away.

The first vivid memory of Mom occurred on a Saturday after breakfast. I went to find her after breakfast with my book in hand. I skipped down the hall, drawn to the gospel music resounding from the parlor. I stood in the doorway and looked at Mom gazing out the window. Illuminated in sunlight, she sat in her favorite blue and white checkered chair in a soft blue robe. Her beauty took my breath away. I dashed over to her with my book. "Mom, read to me." I placed my book in her limp, open hands only to watch it fall to the floor.

"Mom? Mom?" I looked up at her beautiful, empty eyes fixated out the window. I squeezed and shook her lifeless hands over and over again to get her to notice me. "Mom!" Panic gripped my heart. I released her hands and backed away. Instantly, I felt Zafarrah's hands under my arms gathering me into hers.

"Darla, I'm here." Zafarrah looked into my eyes and wiped away my tears.

"What's wrong with Mom?" I asked.

"She's away in her thoughts, like the pretend games we play."

"Why does she pretend by herself?" Through my tears I stared at Mom's shell across the room.

"Sometimes big people get their hearts hurt so bad that their minds play pretend without telling anyone, even them." She held me close and patted my back as we left the room. "This pretend game is a sickness in her mind. We must leave her alone when she pretends."

Who hurt her? I wanted Mom to read to me, to be with me. "Can't we fix her?"

"Mr. Sam asks me to play Jesus music to sing to her heart. Maybe your God can fix her through music." She smiled. "She will come back and have good days, the way she colored with you yesterday. Remember?" I nodded my head.

"Come with me," Zafarrah whispered and carried me to my room. We set up my play table for a tea party. "You can be my little one and I will be your Madar and take care of you. I won't leave you," she smiled at me with her six front teeth above the tea cup in her hand. "Let's play tea party and be happy." Zafarrah had been and would continue to be the mother who fed me, dressed me, laughed with me, and dried my tears. Zafarrah was the mother who cherished me. Our love and bond grew deeper with each passing year.

*   *   *

When I was five, Zafarrah took me on great adventures at the open market to buy our food every other day. She hid me under her robe for extra protection because Americans were often kidnapped.

Under her loose woven black robe, I walked in front of her with the back of my head resting on her stomach. I felt safe and protected with super invisibility powers. I could choose to view the world concealed under the semi-sheer mesh robe or I could peek out to see the world unobstructed. I was told Zafarrah and all other women had to keep themselves covered from head to toe with these robes or they would be killed with stones. Only their eyes were allowed to be visible to others. Her robe kept us safe from the world and bound to each other.

As we walked in unison around the corner, my nose was assaulted by the stench of dead fish displayed on wooden crates. Flies covered their bulging eyes inches from my face. My tummy churned from the putrid odor emitted from the arms and legs of dead lambs, goats, and chickens strung up on poles, baking in the sun, waiting to be purchased and eaten. Across the aisle from the aroma of death I saw frisky young lambs, goats, and chickens eating and pooping, full of life.

"It smells horrible, Zafarrah," I whispered and pinched my nose.

"Yes, the smells of life and death are part of the market and our lives." Zafarrah filled her large bag with a leg of lamb. She was careful not to expose my presence. "Now let's find spices and bread." She turned us toward the next aisle. It was an abstract mural created by the scattered colors and textures of beautiful rugs, cloths, and brass and

6

silver bowls displayed on walls, stakes, crates, and tables. High-pitched rhythmic chants replaced the animal sounds. The delicious smell of fresh baked flatbread combined with aromatic spices overpowered the stink of the animals the farther we walked. After Zafarrah loaded her basket with goodies, we wandered through the rest of the market talking and laughing before we headed home. Zafarrah helped me navigate through the market and my life. She was my angel Madar.

Chapter 3

"What you see and hear depends a good deal on where you are standing; it also depends on what kind of a person you are."
—C. S. Lewis

I can't recall if Mom got better or if age helped me adapt and recognize when she was present. Mom's periods of awareness allowed me to ask her questions about life. My first questions revolved around the differences I observed between my brother and me. I asked her why Conner didn't go to the market like I did.

She explained the world consisted of many groups of people. We lived in Iran with the Persian group, Dad and Conner were Irish from Ireland, and she and I were Native Americans from a group in America. Each group of people had a similar language, color of skin, hair, and eyes that linked them together.

"Conner has red hair and blue eyes and he looks like Daddy, and I have brown hair and brown eyes and I look like you." I remarked.

"Yes, you and I resemble several groups. We can dress the way they do and blend into the scenery like the lizards that change colors," she paused, wrinkling her forehead. "The bad people take children and sell them for money or demand money for their return. That's called kidnapping. Because you blend in, you probably wouldn't be taken. But Conner's red hair, blue eyes, and light skin are a beam of light against the Iranian group of dark skin, eyes, and hair. If they took him, they would get more money for him. They think he's more valuable and special, so we need to keep a closer guard on him."

"I want red hair and blue eyes, Mom. I want to be special." I tilted my head.

"God picked how you look. He has his own plan for you. You'll see." She hugged me to make me feel better, but it didn't work.

What plan? I want to be special and more valuable. Maybe if I asked God to make my eyes blue and make me special, He would. But if He does, I could get taken. This problem had no solution in my little girl mind. I moved my attention to deal with my everyday life.

*   *   *

Conner was constantly on the go and took most of my parents' time and energy. He'd disassemble his toys and mine to see what was inside, how they worked, and if he could put them back together. I played with my dolls, toys, books, and Zafarrah.

One afternoon I watched Conner run through the room in his Superman cape. I asked Mom why he never sat still.

"He's hyperactive. It's an illness that makes him want to continually move, like having an extra engine inside of him. He can't help himself," she explained.

"Is that why he takes medicine?" I asked.

"Yes," Mom said.

"Is that why you take medicine? I want to take medicine too," I said.

"No, you don't. Now quit being silly and go outside and play." She pushed me toward the patio door.

Why can't I join them? Why am I so different? I questioned on my way outside to our small sunken cement wading pool. I reached the pool to see Conner with a large plank of wood, a hammer, and three long nails he'd hauled out of the shed. "Conner, what are you doing?"

"I'm building a diving board and you can help, Sissy." He grinned.

"Okay." I jumped into the pool and held the board steady. Conner hammered and hammered and hammered. He managed to get two of the nails in at the edge of the pool.

"Okay, Darla, I'll let you jump first." He stood on the nailed end of the plank.

I shook my head. "No way. You go first."

He walked out to the end of the board. "Okay, I'll go first." He began to jump and laugh. Suddenly, a loud crack rang out and one of the large nails shot through the air, planting itself in the top of Conner's head.

"Conner, you're a Martian with one antenna," I laughed.

"Ahh," he screamed and looked at me in horror.

Blood gushed down his head and I panicked. I ran into the house to find help. I burst into the parlor. "Mom, Conner's a Martian!" I pointed to him as he ran in the door behind me. Mom screamed for Zafarrah and everyone scuttled around to contain Conner and get him to the hospital. A few hours and stitches later he was back home, on the move again.

Several days later, Conner repeatedly asked Mom to read to him. She was tired and called for Daddy to come help her. He was at a tea party with me and Zafarrah. "Darla, I need to go downstairs. You understand." Daddy patted me on the head and smiled as he left.

"I understand Conner hogs Mom and Daddy and I want my turn,"

I cried to Zafarrah.

"I'm here, Darla. It's okay." Zafarrah wiped my tears.

I heard Daddy yell at Conner to slow him down. This had the opposite effect. "Zafarrah, please come down and help us," Dad pleaded.

"Darla, I must go." Zafarrah rushed off.

I snuck down the hall to see Conner darting around the room. Dad and Zafarrah tried to calm him down while Mom sat in a chair and stared out the window, unmoved by the chaos. Conner had everyone with him. He ruined my tea party and I was left alone again. I exited the commotion on a mission to find Conner's beloved Matchbox cars. I clomped to his room in my cowboy boots and pink ruffled dress. I gathered all the cars I could find, bundled them in the front skirt of my dress, and headed to the storage closet in the hall where Daddy kept our fix-up tools. With one hand clutching a hammer and the other holding my skirt, I released the cars from my skirt. I leaned down and placed the hammer on the floor to line up the cars in a pretty row. With shrieks of joy I raised the hammer and put each car through my custom crusher. My demolition noise and yelps of delight soon brought everyone running. Instead of good attention, I was sent to my room for punishment, isolation, and abandonment, again. In my five-year-old mind I couldn't understand why this didn't work the same for me. I waited for everyone to leave, then I snuck out of my room with Tatters, my one true stitched friend.

Tatters had always been in my life. I was told she was given to me at birth. She had a bright orange coat and a blue bonnet with patches. Her braids stuck out of the bottom of her bonnet to reveal her blonde hair. She had red and white striped socks and black shoes. I especially loved her big eyes that resembled mine. Besides Zafarrah, Tatters had been the only constant companion and love I trusted in my short life. I believed she loved me and I loved her. Nothing could ever separate us. Whenever I was sad or hurt, she helped me through the pain. When my heart ached I often retreated with her to my secret place, my tiny nook deep under the staircase, just big enough for Tatters and me. I was safe and in control in my little space. No human could touch me, hurt me, or leave me.

Chapter 4

"Why love if losing hurts so much?
We love to know that we are not alone."
—C. S. Lewis

My sixth birthday meant I could go to school with my brother. We would wait at the door for the guards in a white, unmarked, windowless van to pick us up and escort us to school. The van guards handed us to a lady inside who greeted us with a death grip cheek pinch every morning. I would clasp my face with both hands to deflect the agony, but she was bigger and stronger and she won.

School left me stuck between two worlds. I didn't understand the majority of their words and they didn't understand most of mine. I tried to find a way to communicate, but I was constantly distracted by my instinct to identify who was safe and who wasn't. My excitement for school was hampered by uncertainty and fear.

After several days of school Conner was upset, unusually quiet, and still all the way home. I tried to talk to him but he ignored me. Mom greeted us at the door and Conner ran into her arms. She led him into the parlor. I secretly crouched outside the doorway and strained to hear the source of Conner's tears.

"The kids at school call me bad names and hurt my feelings," Conner sputtered. "They tell me I don't look like you because you aren't my real mom and I don't have a dad. They say I'm bad. Mom, why do they say that? What's wrong with me?"

"There's nothing wrong with you. You're a good boy. They want to make you feel bad because they're jealous that they aren't special," Mom explained.

"I'm special?" Conner said.

"Yes, you're special because you're adopted," Mom replied.

"What's adopted?" Conner asked.

"You had a different mom and dad who lived in Ireland. They made you but they couldn't take care of you. Your Irish parents picked us to take care of you. This is called adoption. The next time someone says mean things to you because you're different, tell them they're jealous because you're special. Tell them, 'my parents picked me but your parents were stuck with you.' Don't let them hurt you. We picked you and we love you."

I gasped and leaned against the wall to catch my breath. I look like Mom. I wasn't picked. My heart throbbed with the pain of sadness and disappointment. I crawled away from the door. I made my way to Tatters in my room. I sobbed. "Tatters, they're stuck with me. I'm not special. Do they love me? Maybe, if I'm a good girl they will keep me. At least you love me." I hugged her tighter and cried myself to sleep.

Sunday I awoke to Dad's songs, scrambled eggs, and Mom's happy chatter. After breakfast we dressed for church at the American Embassy. This was one of the few times we could dress in American clothes and speak to other Americans who worked in Iran in the oil fields and served as missionaries. Church kept us connected to God, each other, and our American identity. I loved to hear the Bible and missionaries' stories of how God healed poor people's broken arms, legs, and eyes. They called these healings miracles of God, the same God my parents talked about, believed in, and sang to at home. Their stories and Dad's songs merged a unified joy in my spirit. I started to see who God was through all of them.

Occasionally my parents welcomed new missionaries into our home for coffee or a meal to help them adjust to the customs of Iran. We loved to have new playmates from America. When the missionaries had children we would run off to our playroom and escape the adults.

One Sunday evening after church, a new missionary family without children came to our house for coffee. Mom asked Conner and me to stay long enough for introductions before bed. This was the first time we didn't have children to flee with so we stayed. Mom introduced Conner. "This is Conner. We adopted him and he's a full-blooded Irishman like his dad." She smiled and hugged him. Then Mom introduced me. "This is Darla. She's our miracle baby because I had lost three others. But when she was born she ripped everything out of me and I've never been the same." She smiled and patted me on the head. "Give us a kiss and off to bed you go."

Numb and in shock I went through the polite motions of goodnights and fled toward the shelter of my room. Tears erupted from my soul. Mom's words vibrated my heart to a pulp with every step. "I ripped everything out of her." I reached my bed and Tatters and collapsed. "I hurt Mom, Tatters. She plays pretend because of me. No wonder I'm not special. I never can be in her eyes. I hurt her. Her illness is all my fault." I curled into a fetal position and clung to Tatters. *No wonder she pretends away from me. How could I ever make up for all her pain? How can I fix her?* I wept until I had no more tears. I rubbed my eyes and sat up. "Tatters, I'm lucky they've kept me after I hurt Mom. Maybe if I take care of her, she can find some way to forgive me, to pick me, to keep me. Maybe someday she will even love me."

*   *   *

Mom had good and bad days. Zafarrah, Tatters, and Conner were the constants in my life. I never knew when Dad would be home until he walked in the door, but I always waited for him.

One afternoon the doorbell rang. A somber man in uniform, hat in hand, reported, "Mrs. Hughes, I'm sorry to tell you your husband's plane exploded on take-off. There were no survivors." Mom collapsed into Zafarrah's arms and sobbed.

"Mom, what's wrong?" I ran and sat beside her and Zafarrah on the floor. Conner followed.

"Conner, Darla," Mom sputtered. "Your daddy's in heaven."

"No, Daddy's not dead. He can't be!" Conner screamed and ran up the stairs to his room and slammed the door.

"Mom. Mom?" I looked into her empty shell, barely responsive.

"Darla, help me take her to bed. She needs to rest and I'll call the doctor," Zafarrah said.

I helped Zafarrah take Mom to her room and tucked her into bed. The clack of Mom's bedroom door latch snapped me to reality. *My daddy's dead.* I ran to my room. Tears streamed down my face. "Tatters, Daddy's in heaven and I won't see him again." I was all alone, swallowed in sadness and fear. I had no daddy and a sick mom. I hugged Tatters and cried. "God, who will take care of me?"

Zafarrah came looking for me and comforted my broken heart by rocking me to sleep. I awoke to see her sleeping in the chair beside my bed. She tried to make our sad days better with extra music and play time. We did our best to play and take care of Mom, who remained in bed several days. On the third day she moved to her favorite chair in the parlor. She listened to Jesus music and cried silently, still far away. I was in the foyer with Tatters, ready to go upstairs to my room and play when the front door opened. My father walked in.

"Hi, Darla. I'm home." Daddy knelt down and held his arms out to me.

I looked at him and froze. He walked toward me. I turned and ran to my secret hiding place under the stairs, afraid to believe he was real. "Tatters, if Dad's real he could go away again and make me sad, and if he's not then it's a ghost." I felt safe in my tiny nook. I didn't mind the darkness; maybe the dark would swallow me and take me to where God was. *Is this where Mom goes in her mind?* My mind raced but I couldn't talk or cry; I was severed from life, inside myself, paralyzed. I remained in my nook and clung to Tatters for two days, unable to respond to the voices of my parents.

In my cocoon, my mind flooded with the story of Bambi that Mom had shared with me last week. When Bambi's mother was killed, I sobbed in Mom's arms. "I don't want you to die and leave me. I want you to get well."

"God alone knows when our time on earth is done. When we trust in God while we are here, He promises to take care of us because He loves us and He keeps His word." She paused and sighed. "If God takes me to heaven, He will send someone to take care of you like He gave you Zafarrah for now. God will never ever leave you when you trust Him."

"How can I trust someone I can't see?"

"You will hear His soft, peaceful voice and feel Him in your heart, and your spirit will recognize and know Him."

In my dark despair, safe in my nook, I closed my eyes and hugged my legs, clutching Tatters next to my heart. "God, where are you?" I whispered.

A blanket of peace surrounded my heart and I heard a soft voice say, "No matter what happens in your life, you will never be alone because you are loved by Me, your God. I am with you always." Mom was right. I knew His voice. From that moment on, no matter what came my way, God would be with me. Without a doubt He was real.

The voices of Zafarrah, Conner, Mom, and Dad grew louder with each breath. My mind pushed through the dark haze to behold the sun's warm glow lighting the way outside my nook. "Tatters, it's a miracle Dad's alive. If I stay in my nook I'll miss the chance to be loved. I shook my head. I don't want to stay here. I need to take care of Mom because I hurt her. Maybe if I'm a good girl I can fix her or I can help her get a miracle." I started out of my nook and found the trail of crunchy cheese curls my family laid out to entice me from my hole. I munched my way out until I spotted my family and ran into their arms.

"Darla, everything's okay." Dad held me tight.

"It's all okay." Mom hugged and kissed me.

"Sissy, I missed you," Conner said. "Let's go play. You can hammer my cars if you don't hide under the stairway again."

Chapter 5

"Love is unselfishly choosing for another's highest good."
—C. S. Lewis

Dad told me the night before the plane crash he got very sick and went to the hospital in the middle of the night. They kept him overnight, which is why he missed his flight and didn't die. He said God let him get sick to spare him from heaven so he could stay with us. He also said it was no longer safe for us in Iran. His words shocked me. I had never felt safe. Dad announced we would move back to America in one week.

All week we gathered and packed our clothes, toys, and books into large boxes. Mom said our treasures would go to America first and they would be delivered to our new home. Two men came and took away the evidence of our lives. We were left with a little furniture and each other for one last night. Before bed, Zafarrah helped me rearrange my small suitcase for our plane trip in the morning.

"Zafarrah, I can't wait to go to America," I said.

"Tomorrow change will come soon enough. Everything has a time. Your time in Iran is over and tomorrow you'll start a new life. Find the good and leave the bad. Get some sleep. I will always love you." Zafarrah gazed in my eyes, kissed my forehead, and left.

"I love you too, Madar." I smiled at her.

"It's morning! Get up! We're off to America on a new adventure!" I shouted, running through the house waking everyone up.

"Dad, what will we see? What will we do? Where will we live?"

Conner asked.

"Slow down, Conner. You'll see a million new things and we'll live near the ocean in North Carolina. "

We dressed and carried our suitcases to the front door. Raheem, our loyal body guard, arrived and loaded our bags into his car one final time.

"Mom, where's Zafarrah's bags?" I asked.

"She's not coming with us." Mom adjusted the zipper on my small bag.

"Why?" I screamed in disbelief and backed away from her.

"She has her own children and she must stay and take care of them," Mom replied.

"No, she has to come." I fell to my knees and wept. My world exploded. Zafarrah had fed, bathed, and cared for me all my life. She made me laugh, hugged me close, and dried my tears. She was the mother I trusted and relied on. She loved me and I loved her. She was the mother of my heart, she was my Madar. "Now who will take care of me?" I cried.

"Don't be silly. We're your parents and we'll take care of you. We always have. Stop crying and give Zafarrah a hug good-bye." Mom pulled me up to my feet and escorted me to Zafarrah, whose face was wet from silent tears.

"Zafarrah, I can't leave you!" I screamed, and jumped into her arms, my heart broken.

"Darla, I will be in your heart and you will be in mine. Nothing will ever separate our love," Zafarrah whispered in my ear and hugged me tighter. "You must go and have a good life. I'll love you forever."

"I love you, Madar." I gave her one last lingering hug and kiss. Dad took my hand and led me away to Raheem's car. I clung to Tatters in utter anguish all the way to the airport, weeping in silence. "God, what will I do without Zafarrah to love me and take care of me when Mom pretends and Dad's gone? I can't count on anyone but you and Tatters. Help me. Zafarrah saved me; she was my angel. Please take care of my Madar Zafarrah. Maybe if I'm good, God, you'll send me another angel. I promise I'll do my best. Please help me."

Chapter 6

"There are only two ways to live your life. One is as though nothing is a miracle. The other is as though everything is a miracle."
—Albert Einstein

Raheem drove us to the airport. We hugged him and said more tearful good-byes. We made our way through the airport and boarded a PanAm airplane headed for Fayetteville, North Carolina, to start our new lives. It was 1970; I was six and Conner was eight. My heart ached from the loss of Zafarrah, but I had to be a good brave girl so my parents wouldn't leave me, too.

As I buckled my seatbelt on the airplane, my heartache was distracted by my fear of an uncertain future. I wondered how America would be. The only two Americans I knew were from the shows I saw in Iran—Daniel Boone and Get Smart. In my mind America had cowboys and Indians in the mountains and plains, and spies and bad people in the cities. Dad said we would live in the city, so I guessed we'd get the spies.

What would our house look like? Would I be safe? What would happen to me? The plane taxied down the runway faster than when I helped Dad taxi his plane to a hangar. The engines revved and vibrated my seatbelt.

"Mom, I'm scared." I hugged Tatters close.

"These noises and vibrations are normal." Mom reached for my hand while the plane shot down the runway. "Hold my hand and take a deep breath. Before you know it we'll be in the sky, near heaven."

The rumbles and high-pitched noises ceased when we left the ground. I looked out the window and watched the city and desert grow smaller and smaller until I saw the ocean. A sense of release elevated my soul the higher we climbed. *Is this how birds and angels feel every time they fly?* I gazed out the window, lost in a new awareness of freedom.

Once the plane leveled off, a stewardess brought my breakfast tray. "Mom, what are these?"

"This is your first grapefruit." Mom pointed to the circle-shaped fruit on the tray. "With a maraschino cherry on top and an apple turnover." Mom smiled.

"Why doesn't it smell like the fruit in Iran?" I asked after my inspection.

"In America we won't have to wash all the fruit and vegetables in the disinfectant we used in Iran to kill the bugs and germs." Mom sprinkled sugar on my grapefruit. "You can smell and taste their natural flavors. Try it. You'll love it."

I scooped the first bite into my mouth. The tart and sweet spurts of juice woke my taste buds to a fresh new flavor. "Yummy, this is good." Sweet and tangy cinnamon apples caressed my taste buds, intermingled with the airy crust layers of my first apple turnover. "These are flakes from heaven. I can't wait to taste more American food." I finished the last flakes and my maraschino cherry and wondered what other great things lay ahead. During the flight the stewardess took Conner and me up to visit the cockpit and gave us crayons and coloring books. Flying was the most fun I'd ever experienced. I settled in my seat and looked out the window while we descended. It was green everywhere, unlike Iran. "Tatters, we're off on a new adventure. Don't worry. I'll never leave you," I whispered.

We landed in Fayetteville, North Carolina, and took a taxi, minus a guard, to find our new home. We drove over clean paved streets outlining small and tall concrete buildings with no walls or razor wire. At the edge of the city the concrete buildings were replaced by rows of houses surrounded by carpets of fuzzy green lawns, free from trash and sewage ditches. We saw hundreds of people walking, running, and riding bikes in every direction. Not one of them was covered in a robe or head wrap. "Where are the guards to protect the children?" I asked.

"You're in America now," Mom explained with a smile. "You don't need to be afraid of everyone and you won't need a body guard. America created rules to allow us to live without fear and to keep us safe. You are free like the birds flying in the sky. You can walk around and play as long as you tell me where you are."

No guards, no hurt, no fear. Is this possible? I never want to leave. I hugged Tatters closer. *I wish Zafarrah were here so she could be free with me.*

"This will be our new neighborhood," Dad declared at the entrance sign of the Sunnyville Trailer Park. We turned one way and another to see rows of long, skinny houses pass by. There were 1,000 trailers in the park. At last we reached 401 Sunflower Drive. Our long, white, skinny box house with blue shutters was called a single-wide trailer. A gigantic truck, "a semi" Dad said, was parked out front with two men waiting to help us move our treasures inside. They had already unloaded our large brown car, a Chevy Impala.

"Okay everyone, let's get out and see our new home," Dad said.

Conner and I ran from the car to the house and waited for Dad to open the door to our new life. Dad and Mom were close behind. "Dolly, we have a fresh start." Dad leaned down to kiss and embrace Mom before he led her through the door. "Your castle awaits you, my queen." Dad smiled and bowed down, flaring one hand upward.

"Oh, Sam, you're so precious." Mom blushed and kissed him.

"Can we see the house or are you two going to keep kissing?" Conner asked.

"Come in and look around, you two." Dad motioned for us to go in.

We stepped into a narrow living room with shaggy dark green carpet. It looked like fur so I reached down to pet it. The kitchen was at the front of the trailer with three bedrooms and two bathrooms located in the back of the trailer. It was tiny compared to our house in Iran, but it was home because we were all together.

"Hello, anyone home?" A man's voice echoed in a distinct rhythm from the front of the trailer.

"Yes, can I help you?" Dad walked from the back bedroom to the living room with all of us close behind him.

"Hi, my name is Jerome and this is my wife Jenny, our daughter Naomi, and son Bobby. We live across the street. We wanted to see if you needed any help moving in?" Jerome said. He extended his hand and smiled.

I grabbed onto Dad's hand, still unsure if I was safe. I saw Naomi and smiled. She returned the smile with the whitest teeth I'd ever seen surrounded by the darkest skin.

"Hi, I'm Naomi and this is Sally." she held out her doll. "Want to play?"

"Yes. My name is Darla and this is Tatters." I grinned and held out Tatters.

"Let's go outside and talk." She grabbed my hand and pulled me toward the front door.

"Where did you come from?" Naomi asked. She took a seat on the edge of the porch and I joined her.

"I came from a far away country where I had guards and walls to keep me safe," I said.

"Why?" Naomi's eyes widened.

"People would kidnap you and sell you to someone and you'd disappear," I said.

"That's not right." Naomi furrowed her eyebrows. "Well, you're in America and safe with me. It's my job to show you how to have fun." She jumped off the porch, grasped my hand, and led me to the yard. We whirled around in circles until we fell, engulfed in laughter.

We lay in the grass and stared at the soft clouds transforming before our eyes just like my life. Naomi jumped up and pulled me to my feet. We returned to our perches on the front porch. She told me about her aunts, uncles, cousins, and grandparents. She described school and the games she liked to play. I shared my life experiences of camel rides, airplanes, jeep rides, and the open market. Naomi told me the neighbors to avoid "because they're mean" and the ones who would help me if I needed it. She was my first friend. We began to talk about America when her parents and brother came out of the house and asked her to go home with them. Mom peeked out the front door and asked me to help her organize the kitchen. Naomi got up to leave.

"Will I see you tomorrow?" I asked.

"Sure, I'll be around. I live in the blue trailer across the street. Bye." She skipped home.

I went inside and helped Mom organize the kitchen for the rest of the afternoon. "Okay, kids, we've unpacked all day and we're too tired to cook," Dad said. "Let's go and eat some fast food."

"What's fast food?" Conner asked.

"It's a place where we go in and order food. They fix it fast and we sit down and eat it," Dad said.

"We're taking you kids to experience the wonderful taste of a cheeseburger at Burger King." Mom licked her lips. "I sure hope they're as scrumptious as I remember before we went to Iran."

We scrambled into our car, hungry and excited to taste more American food. The barrage of smells hit my nose and triggered a flood of saliva in great anticipation of the new flavors in the air as we entered the restaurant. I didn't know food could smell so delicious. We went up to the counter and saw pictures of many meals on the wall.

"Mom, what do we do?" I said, overwhelmed.

"I want those skinny long white colored things." Conner pointed to a picture.

"Okay, kids, I'll order for you. Conner, those are called French fries and they're great. Go with Mom and find a seat. I'll come with the food shortly." Dad turned to place our order and Mom helped us get napkins and catsup packets on the way to our seat.

"Mom, it smells yummy. How long does it take?" I asked.

"It's ready. Dad's coming now," Mom said.

"Wow, that's fast." Conner fidgeted in his chair.

"Here's our food." Dad placed the large tray on the table and handed each of us a cheeseburger and French fry package. All the food was individually wrapped, unlike the food at the market handed to us in flatbread by dirty hands. I watched Mom to see what to do. I copied her and opened the wrapper of my cheeseburger.

"This is like a Christmas present we can eat." I smiled and licked my lips. I leaned over the burger and inhaled the aroma. "It smells great but I don't know where to start." I decided to dismantle my cheeseburger into piles and taste test each ingredient of lettuce, pickle, cheese, hamburger, and onion. "The pickle is sour and the onion burns my mouth, Mom."

"Darla, I know all these ingredients taste strange, but if you put it all back together and try it, you'll love it," she said.

I reassembled it and took a bite. "Oh, yummy." I gobbled down half my cheeseburger before I snatched my first French fry. I dipped the end in catsup and bit it off. The crisp collided with the sweet catsup flavor, bringing delight to my tongue and a smile to my face. I continued to shove fries basted with catsup into my mouth. *I wish Tatters and Zafarrah could taste this terrific food. I'm glad we're in America safe at last. I hope she's okay.*

"Mom, I have to go potty. Where's the bathroom?" I looked around.

"It's over there." she pointed to the right. "I'll take you."

"I'm almost seven. I can go by myself." I stood up and walked toward the bathroom. I reached for the door as a lady came out and she let me in. I went potty and washed my hands. I stopped at the door and reached for the handle only to find a ball. How do I get out? I grabbed the ball and pushed and pulled with my damp, slippery hands. I screamed, "Help! I'm trapped! I can't get out!" I panted and shrieked. *Am I being punished or left? I'm sorry I was bad and hurt Mom. Zafarrah where are you? God, please let me out. I promise I'll be good.* "Someone please let me out." I sobbed and banged on the door unaware I accidently locked it.

"Darla, calm down. You're okay," I heard Mom say from the other side of the prison door.

"Mom, get me out. Help me," I cried.

"Help's on the way," Dad said as the door handle clicked and flew open. A strange lady reached for me and I ducked under her raised arms and ran into Mom's. "Mom, please don't let her kidnap me."

"There's nothing to fear." Mom hugged me. Safe in Mom's arms, I heard applause. I looked around to see the entire restaurant of customers staring at me. I blushed.

"Darla, you're okay." Dad joined in a group hug.

"Mom, where's the door handle?" I wiped my tears.

"In America most of the door handles are round. In Iran they are L-shaped." She pointed to the door knob. "Many things are different in America and you'll learn about them in time."

"Boy, Darla, you sure made a fuss." Conner laughed.

"I didn't mean to." I looked down as we all left the restaurant, clutching Tatters close. "Tatters, will I ever be safe? America's better but I don't have Zafarrah. I'm glad I have you. I hope it's not all this scary," I whispered and held her tight the whole way home.

*   *   *

Moving to America sparked a new joy in Mom. She polished and rearranged our collection of life and made lists of supplies we needed to complete her organizational projects.

"Today we'll visit K-Mart, your first department store," Mom said.

"Come on, kids, let's get in the car. We need to get our shopping done early," Dad said.

"What's a department store?" Conner asked. "A clean indoor market with more stuff than you could dream of. You'll love it." Dad pulled out on the highway and turned up the radio.

Conner and I were enchanted by the words and melodies of rock-n-roll, country, and folk music from the first time we heard them in the American airport. We asked Dad why we didn't hear all these kinds of music in Iran and he told us Iran's government controlled everything to keep their people afraid so they could dominate them. He said music was the evidence of a people's freedom of expression and Iran didn't want its people to feel free. We spent endless hours listening to the radio in our bedrooms and learning the words so we could sing along.

"Dad, can we listen to the Jackson Five or The Three Dog Night or Elvis?" Conner asked.

"Okay, kids, I'll find a rock-n-roll station." Dad turned the radio knob until he found a clear channel.

A variety of rhythms danced out of the car speakers into my joyous heart. "I love freedom." The melodies and words evoked a spastic revolution in my heart, spilling out through my voice and newfound body jerks in the back seat. Conner and I kept singing "ABC, 123" from the Jackson Five as we walked to the entrance of K-

Mart. To our amazement, without human assistance, the door in front of us magically opened.

"Wow, Mom, the door opened like the cave wall in the story of Ali Baba and the Forty Thieves when he said 'open sesame.'" Conner flailed his arms and repeated "open sesame" as if he were in control of the door.

"Yes, it's called an automatic door." Mom laughed and walked us through the magic entrance.

The store was enormous with bright lights and many aisles of food, toys, and clothes of every color of the rainbow. Jumbo carts could carry our supplies or give us rides. I touched everything possible in my four-foot range. I experienced a sensory overload like a six-year-old with four cups of coffee. There wasn't a section of animals that forced me to hold my nose or watch where I stepped. I could touch, walk, and talk without the fear of being discovered and taken away. America was wonderful.

We shopped for hours and I began to get tired. "Mom, can I ride in the cart?"

"Yes, Dad can help you in the basket," she said.

"Sure." Dad lifted me in the large basket.

I sat down and peered through the wire mesh of the cart. Instantly, I was transported to the mesh view from under the protection of Zafarrah's robe. My heart plunged into a pit of sadness. I missed my Madar Zafarrah. Was she was okay? Did she miss me? The hole in my heart and pools of water in my eyes proved I loved her and I missed her. I wasn't silly; I was heartbroken. I cried silently for several aisles. Zafarrah wasn't here to wipe away my tears, but I was. I can't show

Mom or Dad my tears. What if they get mad at me and leave me behind, too? I have to make them happy. They're all I have. Several minutes passed and I wiped my eyes and stood up in my new world, determined to enjoy the rest of my ride. After all, tomorrow was Sunday and we would find new friends at church.

*   *   *

Dad's singing, scrambled eggs, and bacon awakened me. After breakfast I put on my new pink dress, grabbed my little Bible, and headed out the door with my family.

"What's church like in America?" I asked.

"It will be amazing. People will sing in a group called a choir while a band plays instruments." Dad smiled.

"We'll have music in church?"

"Yes. We didn't have it in Iran because the government forbade us to worship. In America we have the freedom to sing and praise God openly," Dad said.

"Will we bring missionaries home?" Conner asked.

"No, we'll make friends and create a family like we did in Iran," Mom said.

We drove to a big white church with a sign on the front that read Fayetteville Pentecostal Church, Everyone Welcome. We parked and climbed several stairs, greeted with smiles and hugs from people who stood by the doors. We walked down the aisle in front of a large mostly black choir seated at the front of the church on stage. Halfway down the aisle we found four empty seats amidst several hundred people. The pastor welcomed everyone and announced the choir director. The director stood up and motioned for the choir to stand. He raised his hands and dropped them. Music exploded simultaneously from the choir, the piano and organ, trumpet, and tambourines. Their detonation vibrated every cell in my body and soul. The choir swayed to the rhythm of the beat, giving life to each word. The music became their life's breath and mine. I tugged on Dad's sleeve and he bent down. "Is this how heaven sounds, Dad?"

"It will be a million times better." He smiled and continued to clap and sing.

The hallelujahs, amens, clapping, and dancing were a celebration of joy I never imagined possible. God was in the air and I wanted to grab Him and hold Him forever. The music stopped and the preacher echoed Mom and Dad's love and understanding of Jesus. He said God made me, He loved me, and He wanted me to live with Him in heaven for eternity. All I had to do was believe Jesus is the Son of God, that He died for all my sins, and that His sacrifice made it possible for me to be forgiven by God. *If I believe and confess my sins and ask Jesus to come into my heart, He will save me.*

I knew without a doubt I needed a savior. "God, I know you spoke to me under the staircase but I need to know for sure that you forgive me for being so bad by hurting Mom. I need to know that you will never leave me." I repeated every word of the preacher's prayer and looked heavenward. An extraordinary downpour of joy filled my being. The choir began to sing and now my joy reflected theirs. We sang a few more songs and then headed home, overflowing with Jesus.

We had lunch and played with our friends outside until dark. Mom called us home and we found Dad sitting on the couch with two large bowls of popcorn, watching TV. "The Wonderful World of Disney is on." Mom pointed to the television and sat next to Dad.

"What's that?" Conner asked.

"It's a television show with funny cartoons this week." Mom reached for a handful of popcorn. "You'll love them. Hurry and sit down, the show's starting."

The show started with a beautiful white castle and fireworks. The sparkling words appeared over a castle written by a fairy named Tinker Bell. A variety of cartoon figures called Mickey Mouse, Donald Duck, Goofy, Pluto, and Chip N Dale filled the screen and our hearts with laughter. We had missed so much locked in Iran. The next show, the Animal World, exhibited lions, zebras, giraffes, and hippos I'd only seen in books. I watched the long legs of the giraffe gallop in the clearing next to the elephants grabbing leaves with their long noses. These new images catapulted me to a new awareness that I knew very little of this great big world I was in.

"Wow, how did God make all these creatures?" I asked.

"He's God." Mom smiled.

"Dad, did Iran keep these shows from us, too?" Conner asked and Dad nodded yes.

"I see all the animals, Mom, but I'm glad they're not in the trailer park," I said, my eyes wide, as I pulled Tatters close.

"You're safe here. It's time for bed." Mom gave me a hug and kiss and I gave one to Dad.

"I'm scared enough without lions roaming around to eat me," I whispered to Tatters on my way to bed.

*   *   *

The weeks passed and I embraced my new freedom with less fear. There were still many differences, but the good surpassed the bad. Dad came home early one afternoon and waved four small green pieces of paper in his hand. "Kids, I have a special surprise for you. I won tickets to see Snow White and the Seven Dwarfs at the movie theater."

"What's a movie theater?" I asked.

"It's a room with an enormous television screen. It will be incredible. Let's go." Dad led us out the door.

We arrived at a big gray building crowded with people. The air was saturated with the aroma of popcorn. We waited in line for our free popcorn and a soda pop that came with the tickets. With our treats in hand, we walked into a large, dim room and found four empty seats. "What's behind the big curtain?" I whispered.

"It's the movie screen," Mom said. As lights dimmed and the music started, the curtains opened to reveal an enormous castle and fireworks, filling the entire wall. Each magical scene of Snow White's life steeped in dramatic melodies filled my soul with laughter, tears, and new hope. Her whole life changed when she escaped her bad stepmother, just like mine did by coming to America. She had the seven dwarfs to care for her and God brought me Zafarrah. Snow White kept singing, doing good for others, and hoping for the best. In the end she was rescued by her Prince Charming. If I copy Snow White, I may get rescued by my prince one day.

Between my salvation and my magical big-screen movie experience, I was on a happy surge full of new hope. I played and sang and enjoyed my family and friends. My joy overflowed from within.

Chapter 7

"In the face of uncertainty, there is nothing wrong with hope."
—Bernie S. Siegel

One Friday afternoon Conner and I were playing in the yard. We spotted Dad driving our new blue Mazda pickup home with a yellow box on wheels attached to it. Dad parked and got out, smiling from ear to ear.

"Dad, what's in the box?" I asked.

"I'll show you." He opened the trunk of the car and held a block of wood in each hand. He carried them to the wheels of the box and placed one under each wheel.

"Dad, can I help?" Conner became his shadow.

"Yes, this is a camper. We'll set it up and pack it full of food and blankets. We're going to the beach tomorrow and we'll sleep in here for a week," Dad said.

"How can we all fit in there?" I asked.

"This is a magic pop-up camper. Watch this." Dad unclamped the top. Conner helped him lift the first side, which extended to the right and then the second side, which stretched to the left. In minutes we had a tent on a box. *It was magic.*

"This is cool, Dad. Can we sleep in it tonight?" Conner jumped around.

"Not tonight. I need your help to load it with supplies for our trip." He unzipped the top tent and opened the small door on the lower box. It was spacious inside our magic tent. The extended sides were beds. Between our beds were a table with hollow benches to store our food and a camp stove.

"Let's get the supplies your mom's piled at the door and load them in here. We'll leave for the beach early in the morning."

"The beach. We've never been to the beach. Yippee!" I shouted.

We ran back and forth several times before we closed the camper and went to bed. The sunrise woke us and we loaded into the car, heading for the beach. Dad turned the radio up and we all sang through our two-hour ride.

We turned onto a small road and within minutes we saw blue waves glistening in the sun. They broke into a white rolling spray as they surrendered to the tan, sandy shore. "The ocean's beautiful. Can we walk to it?" I asked.

"Yes, you'll love it." Dad came to a stop.

Conner and I jumped out of the car and ran to the ocean with Dad close behind us. The constant rhythm of the soft, low rumble of the waves soothed and comforted my soul. The waves appeared to be the breath of the earth moving in and out. For all the comfort and peace it gave me, Conner ran wild. "I love the beach. Can we live here?" I asked.

"No, we can't afford to live at the beach, but we can visit." Dad walked beside me and called for Conner. "Let's go and set up the camper so we can get into our swim suits and play in the water."

"Yeah!" Conner yelled and ran back to the camper with me hot on his trail. We set up the camper, unpacked our car, and put on our swim suits. "Dad, we're ready. Can we go?" I said with a towel and blow-up tube in hand.

"We'll go in a minute. We need to wait for Mom to put on her swim suit." Dad blew into an inflatable raft.

"Mom's swimming?"Conner asked.

"Yes, she loves the ocean," Dad said.

Mom couldn't run or ride a bike because she was too ill. *Will she be okay?* From the look on Conner's face I could see we were both concerned. Mom came out and walked with us to the shoreline. We had never seen her in a swim suit and it was hard not to stare. Mom walked out into the ocean with the raft in her hands. "Darla, do you want a ride?" Mom motioned for me to come to her.

"Yes." The tug of the waves made me nervous as I made my way out to her. They were stronger than any force I had come against. My uneasiness made me determined to stay with Mom to make sure she would be okay. Mom leaned the top half of her body over the raft and held out her hand to me.

"Hold onto the side with your hands and extend your legs out like mine and kick," Mom said. I followed her example and we moved to deeper water.

"Mom, how come you can swim but you can't run or ride a bike?" I questioned.

"In the water I'm weightless and it takes less effort for me to move. I'm not swimming; I'm floating. The ocean gives me a taste of how healthy people feel. It's a blessing for me."

We bobbed around and talked about America until our skin was wrinkled. I helped Mom to the shore. These times with Mom were intimate and unusual. She gave me hope that somewhere deep inside she wanted, needed, and loved me.

After we rested on the shore for a while I noticed the waves stopped and the water began to move out into the ocean. "Dad, what's happening?" I said.

"Two times a day the waves move back into the ocean for a rest. It's called low tide," He stood and pulled me up. "This is one of my favorite times to go treasure hunting. Do you want to go?"

"Yes, I want to find treasure!" I followed him to the water.

"Me too. What's the treasure? Gold? Silver?" Conner ran past me.

"The treasure is beautiful artworks of the ocean: sea shells." Dad walked farther and farther out without the water getting deeper. He bent down once in a while to the ocean floor and yelled, "I found one!" He pulled up a white, flat, round, coin-shaped shell with a star on one side. "This is a sand dollar." Dad also extracted a conch shell and a cone shell from the ocean floor and put them in his pocket.

Conner and I found several shells before we saw the waves rolling toward us. We walked back to the shore and rested before we built sand castles. For dinner we caught crabs and roasted marshmallows over the campfire for dessert as it grew dark. We were the Cleavers on TV, a happy family, a dream I never wanted to end.

At dawn Dad and I woke up early to search for more shells that washed ashore during the night before we had to go home. We spotted a large conch shell at the water's edge. A lady ran toward it yelling, "It's mine, it's mine!" She swooped it up. Suddenly she screamed and tossed the shell skyward. The tentacles of an octopus crawled down her arm, dropped to the sand, and scurried out to sea. She ran for her life. The spastic display of flinging arms, legs, and tentacles brought tears of laughter to Dad and me. We wiped the tears from our eyes and went back to camp to share our hilarious story over breakfast.

We reluctantly packed up and climbed back into the car. I sat quietly in the back seat for most of the way home, lost in my thoughts. *Tatters, I love the beach. I want to stay here forever but I know we can't. I will hold on to this good memory, like Zafarrah said, until we come back.*

Chapter 8

"Everything must have a beginning . . . and that beginning must
be linked to something that went before."

—Mary Shelley

My family settled into a new routine over the next few weeks. Having Mom and Dad present gave me a glimpse of what other friends experienced all their lives, a feeling of assurance.

One Sunday after lunch, Dad sat between Conner and me on the couch. He said he needed to talk with us. My heart sank. "Kids, I don't know how to tell you this, but I have to go away for nine months to work on airplanes in the Vietnam War." Dad hugged us tight.

"Why?" I cried. "You can't go."

"Dad, don't go," Conner begged.

"It's my job. You kids will have to take care of your mom and each other, and she'll do her best to take care of you." Tears ran down his face.

"I hate your job and Vietnam!" I shouted, and pulled back from him.

"Darla, I understand you're sad and scared, but I still have to go. It's my job." Dad looked into my eyes. "I have to go and fight for their freedom from the bad guys. Don't you agree we all deserve to be free?"

"Yes, but they can send someone else," I cried.

"Living in a free country makes us responsible to help those who aren't free." He pulled me close. "I'm sorry. I have to go, so let's fill our last days together with love and fun, okay?"

Dad tried to make us laugh and have fun, but our impending pain choked any hint of joy. I didn't understand why American troops were in Vietnam and from what other adults said, they didn't either. I was grateful and cherished the new freedom I enjoyed living in America. I wanted everyone to have it. I just didn't want Dad to leave again. What if he didn't come back this time? I couldn't stop him. At least this time we were safe in America, but we had no one to help us with Mom.

Tuesday morning we dressed in our Sunday clothes and took Dad to the airport. Slumped in the back seat with Conner, I held Tatters close.

"Kids, I'll be okay. God is with us and He will take care of us." Dad pulled into the airport parking lot. He parked the car, got out, and walked to the trunk.

"I don't want to see Dad leave. I'm staying here." I crossed my arms.

"Darla, you can't stay in the car. You must think of Dad." Mom got out of the car and opened the back door where I was sitting. She pulled at my hand while Dad grabbed his duffle bag from the car's trunk. "Dad needs to see you and tell you good-bye. Don't be selfish. This is hard for all of us. Come on." She began to pull me out of the car.

Conner reached for my other hand that clutched Tatters to my heart. "Come on, Sissy," he coaxed, pulling me out of the car.

Dad knelt down beside me. "Darla, I'll come back. You can hear my voice on the cassette tapes and I can hear yours every week. I'll be

42

with you in spirit."

My mind raced. I didn't want to just hear his voice or feel his spirit with me. I needed and wanted him in the flesh. What if he didn't come back?

"I need you to be a big brave girl and take care of Mom and Conner while I'm gone." Dad hugged me.

"Okay, I will." I cried, and melted into Dad's arms. "I love you, Dad. Please come back. Please." I sobbed and Conner joined us.

Dad gave us all one last hug and kiss. He heaved his duffle bag over his shoulder and walked through the door to board the plane. Dad disappeared and we clung to Mom and cried. We watched Dad's plane take off and walked to the car, encased in fear and uncertainty. Mom drove us home in silence. I retreated to my room, to Tatters. The familiar black sadness from under the staircase reached for me again. "God, please bring my dad home, please," I pleaded. My plea to God illuminated the darkness and my hope. God chased away my fears and gave me a new determination to see and make the best of my life.

Mom disappeared into her books, TV, and personal pretend games for several weeks. Conner and I took care of her and each other. We had fun being grownups, cooking hot dogs, macaroni and cheese, and scrambled eggs while perched on a chair. Each week Mom let me help her put little round, oval, and square dots of color in a large container she called her pill box. I took good care of Mom. She called for me. She needed me. I had to be doing something right because Mom became present more and more.

One evening Mom told us she was going to get a job. She would babysit DeeDee, the neighbor's two-year-old little girl, five days a week until school started. Her parents would drop her off early in the morning and pick her up at 5:00 p.m.

"Why do you have to babysit?" I squinted.

"We need extra money since Dad's gone, and DeeDee needs someone to take care of her," Mom said.

"Are we adopting her?" Conner asked.

"No, we'll give her back at night. That's why it's called babysitting. This will be fun for all of us; you'll see. It will be like having a little sister part-time." Mom smiled with delight.

Will Conner and I have to take care of her when Mom can't? DeeDee may have needed someone, but why did it have to be my Mom? I needed her, especially since Zafarrah was gone. Why can't Mom take care of me more?

DeeDee came before sunrise. I peeked out of my room to see Mom carry her to bed with her. *Why did DeeDee get to sleep with Mom when Conner and I weren't allowed to because we might hurt her?* I tried to go back to sleep but the pain in my heart kept me awake.

A couple of hours later Mom carried DeeDee out of her room to the kitchen. Mom was smiling and talking weird to her. She greeted Conner and me and fixed eggs and toast for our breakfast. I searched for a reason why DeeDee seemed to give Mom more joy than I did and I realized DeeDee hadn't hurt Mom. On the days DeeDee wasn't there, my brother and I would fix our own cereal and eat it at the kitchen table. We would make Mom a bowl of cereal and take it to her in bed because she was too tired to get up. I watched Mom hold, hug, and play with DeeDee for hours. I asked Mom to play with me, but she

44

said DeeDee needed her more because she was so small and beautiful. The sight of their love slashed at my heart. I strained to remember Mom showing the same devotion and love to me. I could only see Zafarrah holding and loving me when I was young. Mom wasn't etched in my mind and heart until I was older. "Zafarrah, I need you. I miss you," I whispered and ran to Tatters in my room. "Tatters, I wish Mom could love me the same way." I sobbed until my tears were dry. I colored to get my mind off of my pain. In my few years of life I realized I couldn't change Mom's love for me. All I could do was find a way to be happy somewhere inside.

I heard Mom call for me. I grabbed Tatters and darted to the living room. "Darla, come and play with DeeDee. She's so much fun." Mom motioned for me to sit with them among a pile of toys.

I reluctantly sat down and began to play with DeeDee. She reached for Tatters. "No, she's mine." I rescued Tatters from her hands, knocking her off balance. She fell backwards and cried. Mom embraced DeeDee and cuddled her in her lap. I leaned back and held out my hands. "I didn't mean to hurt her. I was saving Tatters. DeeDee has you and I won't let her have Tatters, too," I said.

"Darla, you're acting like a green-eyed jealous monster. You need to stop being selfish and tell her you're sorry." Mom shook her finger at me.

"I'm not a monster, and I don't have green eyes!" I shouted.

"When you are angry and mean to someone because they have what you want you are being a green-eyed jealous monster." Mom glared at me. "God asks us to share and have a happy heart and not to be jealous."

Mom was right. I was angry and jealous, angry and sad for all the time she was not with me, for all the hours I missed in her arms, and at myself for ever being born. *She gives her love to DeeDee and she says I'm a monster. She's mad at me and God must be mad at me too. Why wouldn't He be?* I began to cry.

"Darla, you have no reason to be jealous." She looked into my eyes. "I have you the rest of the time. You need to learn to share me and be happy for others. There's never a reason to be mean, ever."

I jumped up and ran outside. "God, I don't want to be a monster. Please help me be good and help Mom love me a little."

I did my best to avoid Mom and DeeDee during the day and neither seemed to mind. I looked forward to the evenings and the weekends when Mom needed me to take care of her.

Saturday came and Mom felt good. She wanted to treat us to another big screen movie, "Cinderella." We bought popcorn and a drink and settled into our seats. Oh, how I related to Cinderella. Her stepmother loved her stepsisters more and she treated them better. Cinderella wanted to be loved, but she couldn't make her stepmother love her. She did her best to take care of them and found some love and help through the animals. I had an angel helper in Zafarrah, but now I was all alone. Cinderella and Snow White both kept hopeful, joyous hearts no matter what came their way and they were rescued in the end. The enchantment of a "happily-ever-after" summoned my heart and soul from deep within. "Mom, can I have a Prince Charming some day?" I asked.

"Yes, your dad's mine. Anything's possible if you believe." Mom smiled on our way out the door.

I lay in bed and stared out the window up at the stars. *Maybe if I choose to be happy and have a song in my heart, my life will turn out like Cinderella's.* "Tatters, I believe." I drifted off to sleep.

*   *   *

I loved to go to Sunday school and learn about God. One lesson was about Joseph. His brothers were so jealous of him that they sold him into slavery. Joseph was imprisoned and treated unfairly but he chose to trust and believe that God would take care of him. In time God made him the second boss of Egypt and he saved his family and many others from starvation. On the way home I thought about the similarities between Joseph, Snow White, and Cinderella. They all kept hope and good attitudes and everything ended happily. "God, help me take care of others with a great attitude no matter what so one day I'll be loved, like Joseph, Snow White, and Cinderella," I whispered to Tatters.

Chapter 9

"Crying is all right in its way while it lasts. But you have to stop sooner or later and then you still have to decide what to do."
—C. S. Lewis

The summer ended and Mom quit babysitting DeeDee to prepare us for school. She said school would be easier here because everyone spoke and understood English and all of our friends in the trailer park would be there. I wanted to believe her words but I kept some hope guarded in case she was wrong. Conner and I dressed in our new clothes and Mom drove us to our first day of school. After this day, we would ride the bus with our friends. I was relieved to hear America didn't have a van with a cheek pincher to greet us every morning.

"I'm scared," I whispered on my way to class, holding Mom's hand.

"You have nothing to fear. Be yourself and treat others kindly." Mom hugged me and guided me inside my classroom.

My teacher was Mrs. Johnson. She had black hair and pointy black glasses resembling cat's eyes. "Class, this is Darla. She moved from a foreign country called Iran." She smiled. "Everyone make her feel welcome."

Everyone said hello in unison. I recognized several friends from Sunnyville Trailer Park and I felt more at ease. My introduction triggered the curiosity of several other girls. During recess they asked me about my life and adventures and wanted to be my friend. I hoped I could fit in.

Each week revealed the truth; I had very few similar life and world experiences in common with anyone who had grown up in America. They all talked about President Kennedy, Martin Luther King, Jr., Elvis, and the Vietnam War. These didn't exist in my mind or reality until weeks or months ago. It was as if I had amnesia for seven years and woke up in the middle of a movie. I tried to bridge the gaps, but I remained on the outside struggling to find a door inside.

The simplest things uncovered my uniqueness. I finished my assignment early and took it to Mrs. Johnson, who was rearranging a bookcase at the back of the room.

"Mrs. Johnson, here's my assignment." I extended it to her in my hand.

"Darla, please go to my desk and put your assignment in the left basket," Mrs. Johnson said.

I glanced at her desk. There were two baskets. I froze with fear and moved closer to her. She leaned down to me. "Mrs. Johnson, I don't know which way is left," I whispered.

"This way's left." Mrs. Johnson smiled and waved her left hand. "And this way's right." She waved her right hand.

The desk closest to us was occupied by Tommy Franklin, the class bully. "You don't know your right from your left?" Tommy laughed loudly. "I bet you don't know which way is north, south, east, or west either, you weirdo." Tommy's announcement caught the attention and laughter of the other kids.

"Class, that's enough," Mrs. Johnson blurted out and stood up. "We will not be mean to anyone. We're all different and we will be nice. Now, everyone apologize."

"We're sorry, Mrs. Johnson," the class echoed.

Their words bounced off the daggers in my heart. In Iran I knew where I was by landmarks. *I wish I wasn't different and didn't feel stupid. Why are they being nice one minute and mean the next? Maybe Iran was better. At least I couldn't understand or feel the sting of their words when I messed up.* School pressed on and I strived to remain invisible to avoid more embarrassment and pain. I became an expert at flying under people's radar.

In the spring an eye doctor came to school to give us a quick eye test. Mom received a call from him requesting an exam for me. I asked her if it would hurt and she said the eye doctor was the nicest one of all. I had never been to an eye doctor before and I was relieved to hear her news, yet apprehensive.

We arrived at the doctor's office filled with hundreds of frames for glasses in various shapes and colors. He took us to a room and sat me in a tall chair with a big telescope attached to it. I looked through two round holes with pieces of glass in them. After several clicks and changes of the round glass holes I peered through, the letters on the wall magically appeared crisp and clear. "Mom, I can see." Was this a miracle the missionaries talked about? The room appeared larger than I remembered walking in just a few minutes earlier. I discovered instruments on the counter and flowers on the wallpaper I had thought were dots. The doctor said I should have had glasses at the age of two because I had astigmatism or football-shaped eyes. He said glasses would fix my sight. Mom took me to the room filled with frames. I tried on several frames until I picked a pointy pair like Mrs. Johnson's. I hoped my choice would make her popularity transfer to me.

Through my glasses I saw the world on a big movie screen instead of a small fuzzy TV. For a week the tidal wave of information and images made me dizzy until my eyes and stomach settled into agreement. My new eyesight brought history, geography, and art to a new plateau at school. The words from books sparked a hunger to read and learn all the time. Mom always said knowledge was power and everything I needed to know was in a book, especially the Bible. With my new eyesight, I could find that out for myself. I wanted to know what drew Mom to read and learn. Was it her glasses, too?

"Mom, why do you love books?" She glanced up from a book on Egypt.

"I used to read when I was a little girl and lived on the reservation." She placed the book in her lap.

"What's a reservation?" I asked.

"Long ago our people roamed free all over the United States and took care of ourselves. There were no white people here. They came to America on a ship from England and other parts of Europe. Their government leaders gathered all the different tribes of Native Americans and put them on areas of land called reservations to contain them.

"What did we do wrong?" I looked at her.

"We were different and lived on the land they wanted. They decided to take the land by force instead of finding a way to live together." She sighed. "They didn't treat us right, but they had more power and more people so they won."

"Are people locked on these reservations?" I asked.

"No, there are no solid brick walls like we had in Iran. They are invisible, which is worse." She leaned back in her chair. "If our people left the reservation they were hurt or killed. They learned it was best to stay inside their invisible prison."

"That's not right." I shook my head. "America's the land of the free."

"No, it wasn't right. It's part of our past and when we learn from it we can be better people." Mom patted my leg. "Anyway, when I was a little girl I started to read and it took me away from all the bad things that happened to our people, my family, and me. Books released my imagination. I escaped to pretend worlds where I could explore, conquer, find love, and live the life I'd dreamed about instead of the hard life I had. My life's better because of books."

"I didn't know you had such a bad childhood. Mom, I'm sorry." I squeezed her hand.

"It's okay, look at me now," she said.

Mom smiled but I knew she still felt trapped or she wouldn't have to keep escaping. *There has to be a book I can read to find a way to fix Mom or myself. I'll keep reading until I find it.*

My passion to read and playing with friends also uncovered the reality that our family was different from theirs. Their families had cousins over to play or an aunt, an uncle, or grandparent around. I had no recollection of any family in my past. "Mom, why don't we have aunts, uncles, cousins, or grandparents?"

"You do but they all live in California, clear on the other side of America." Mom looked down.

"How come we don't visit them?" I tilted my head.

"All your grandparents except my Mom, your grandmother, are in heaven." She hesitated. "You have two aunts, seven uncles, and many cousins." She sat down and motioned for me to sit with her.

"Remember when I described our reservation?" Mom looked into my eyes.

"Yes. You said you had a hard life. Why?" I saw sadness in Mom's eyes.

"My side of the family has problems because they drink too much alcohol. Alcohol is a liquid drug that makes some people mean, like my parents." Mom inhaled and sighed. "They've tried to stop, but they haven't been successful. It's not safe to be around them."

"Where's Dad's family?" I asked.

"They're busy with their own lives in California. That's why we create a family wherever we go." Mom smiled. "Darla, all we've ever had is each other and our church family. It's been more than enough, hasn't it?"

"I guess." I went to my room. I hadn't known the missing parts of my family until now. So why did I feel this weird loss? If our family had been around, it wouldn't have been safe or they probably wouldn't have stayed. Maybe it's best they weren't there. "Tatters, at least I have you." I pressed her to my heart. She was the only one I could trust to be here for me. I loved her and she comforted me with her every thread. I didn't have a close family but I had Tatters, Conner, and Mom for now. We did our best to take care of each other while we waited for Dad to come home.

*   *   *

Dad was right—his voice and songs on the tapes eased our fears and closed the miles between us. Our weekly cassette tape arrived and we sat around the kitchen table, anxious to hear Dad's voice. "Kids, I love you. The war's over and I'm coming home for good. I'll see you all soon." These were the only words on the tape.

"Dad's coming home, Darla! Dad's coming home!" Conner cheered and jumped around the room.

Tears ran down my cheeks. "Darla, what's wrong?" Mom touched my hand.

"What if he doesn't make it? What if his plane explodes? " I cried and fell into Mom's arms.

"I understand your fear because of the past." Mom stroked my hair. "I can't promise he'll come back because some things are out of our control. I know Dad's plan is to come home and when he arrives I want him to find a family who's happy to see him." She looked into my eyes. "You can't let the past crush your future happiness. Let's pick out the dress you want to meet Dad in tomorrow."

"Tomorrow?" I pulled away and stared at her.

"Yippee!" Conner shouted and hopped up and down.

"The tape took two weeks to get here. Dad timed the news so we wouldn't have to wait very long. We'll pick him up tomorrow." Mom smiled.

My mind flip-flopped between being happy and scared until I decided I would have Cinderella's happy outlook. I laid my clothes out and drifted off to sleep. The morning sunshine beamed through the window and woke me. We ate breakfast, dressed in our Sunday clothes, and left for the airport. Mom was stunning dressed in a sky blue linen dress with matching high heels and red lipstick. We parked the car and walked through the airport to Dad's exit gate.

"Mom, I can't see him." Conner circled around us and surveyed the crowd.

"Kids, he'll come down this hall." Mom pointed straight ahead. "Look, there he is."

"Dad, Dad!" Conner and I shouted. Our squeals of joy reached Dad's ears and he turned to look at us. He knelt down and braced for impact with open arms. Conner and I ran and engulfed him with our hugs of love. "Oh, how I love you kids," he cried and hugged us. Mom walked over to us and Dad stood up and embraced her. He kissed Mom gently and wiped away her tears. They walked hand in hand to the car with Conner and me at his side. Dad came home alive. He was in the driver's seat, heading toward home.

We were excited to have Dad home and to be a family. Deep inside I wondered when he would leave us again because of his job. Each of Dad's departures chopped at the shield of protection I'd created to never feel the dark devastation and abandonment I'd felt under the staircase in Iran. Keeping the hope and joy of Snow White and Cinderella alive was becoming a full-time endeavor. It didn't seem this hard for them but it was for me, especially at times like these.

A week passed and Dad announced he was retiring from the Air Force. He said retirement meant he would find a job that would let him come home every night and not make him have to go away anymore. Dad said he and Mom would pray and ask God for the right job and God would direct them. He also told us we were all going to the beach for the next two weeks. We swam, ate crabs, and loved on one another at our beach oasis. Both parents were present in their minds, bodies, and spirits. I wanted to extend the only time in my life when I felt loved by my parents and a part of my family. I wished we would never leave. Deep inside I knew this wish wouldn't come true. Nevertheless, I was determined to hope for the best.

Several weeks later we were all in the living room and Mom announced our future. "Last night I had a dream from God. He told me we are to move west toward the Rocky Mountains."

"Mom, how do you know it's from God?" I asked.

"The dream was specific, peaceful, and my heart knows God's voice. The voice told me to have Dad make a 'For Sale' sign and put it in the east front window of the trailer today. Dad won't put the price on the sign. A man will come to the door with $4,509.00 in cash. His money will confirm this message is from God. We are to obey God and let Him do the rest."

"Will we live in the mountains, Mom?" Conner asked.

"God told us to head west and He will tell us when to stop. He's letting us have an adventure if we agree to trust and listen to Him, like Moses." She smiled and asked us to go and play.

I sat on the front step and thought of how much Mom was like Moses. She had a direct line to God and often heard from Him. Now she was leading us on an adventure that made me excited and uneasy because Moses and his people wandered around for forty years. I had also heard God's voice and I hoped He would continue to speak to me when I got older. For now, I wanted to know where we would live. Would I finally fit in? I didn't have these answers and I decided to stick close and be very good so I wouldn't get lost along the way.

Early in the morning a man knocked at the door and we all

gathered around. "Hello, my name is Howard Roland. I saw your For Sale sign in the window, and I want to buy your trailer. I only have $4,509.00 in cash. Will you take it?"

For an instant we all froze and gawked at the man, wide eyed. "Yes, we will. We will. Praise the Lord." Dad smiled and shook Howard's hand. Howard was startled. Dad stepped outside to finish talking to Howard while we celebrated inside.

"We're going west!" Conner and I whooped and hollered. *God did what Mom said He would. Wow, I want to hear from God like that.*

Chapter 10

"Now faith is confidence in what we hope for and
assurance about what we do not see."
—Hebrews 11:1

The next week we packed all our belongings in boxes and loaded them in a semi that would take them to Colorado and store them until we got there. Once the semi left, I buckled into the front seat of our brown Impala with Mom. Conner rode with Dad in our blue Mazda truck, pulling our mighty pop-up camper. We drove our mini-caravan by day and camped in KOA campgrounds at night. Every day amazing new sights and sounds were unveiled, in the thick woods, misty lakes, roaring rivers, and the hundreds of towns and cities America presented to us. America was gigantic, breathtaking, bountiful, and free. We looked forward to seeing the Rocky Mountains and our new home. Daily we'd ask Mom if we were West. She'd smile and say, "No, God will tell us in his time and we must be patient."

We crossed the Colorado border and by dusk began to see mountains. Dad pulled into a KOA campground near Loveland, Colorado, and parked in a camper space. Dad and Mom got out of the car and faced the mountains. "Kids, we're west," Mom announced.

"How do you know?" I asked.

"I saw this view in my dream." Mom pointed to the mountains.

"Where will we live?" Conner set the blocks under the wheels and helped Dad set up the camper.

"We'll stay here until God gives me the next set of directions,"

Mom said.

"When will God give them to you?" Conner asked.

"I'm not sure." Mom shrugged her shoulders. "We need to be patient and have fun while we wait." We made our beds, then Mom and Dad kissed us goodnight and tucked us into bed.

Dad left at sunrise every morning to look for work. He made enough money at odd jobs to keep us fed. Conner and I ate breakfast and ran off to explore our temporary home. The campground had a pool, a park, and a movie night. Best of all, there were many kids to play with. I made friends, laughed, and enjoyed the happiness we found in the West. I hoped life would stay joyous, but deep inside I kept a part of me detached for protection, for survival, when my life encountered its next change.

"Darla, do you think we'll hear from God soon?" Conner asked as we splashed in the pool one August afternoon.

"I sure hope so." I reclined in the sun. "It would be nice to have a house before school starts."

"I'll miss the pool." Conner gathered his towel and float raft and motioned for me to follow.

"Me too." We ran back to the camper to find Mom in a lawn chair immersed in Jonathan Swift's_Gulliver's Travels. "Mom, have you heard from God yet?" I huffed, out of breath.

"Not yet." she smiled. At sunrise Conner and I awoke to the whispers of Dad and Mom. We knew life was about to change again.

"What did you hear?" Conner jumped out of bed.

"Where will we live?" I joined him.

"Kids, calm down." Mom held up her hand. "Let's get dressed

and have breakfast and I'll tell you what I heard." We gobbled our breakfast in record time. Mom cleared her voice. "Sam, I've laid your clothes out on our bed for your job interview today. You need to drive three miles west and two miles north and you'll see a new school being built. Go into the office and request to speak with Mr. Cooper and ask him for a job. Once you have the job, go one mile west and turn right. You'll see a farmhouse. That's our new home."

"Okay, honey." Dad stood up and kissed Mom on his way back into the camper. Dad sang while he dressed. He came out of the camper, hopped into his pickup, and headed off on his quest. Dad never debated or questioned Mom when she delivered a message from God. He obeyed.

"What should we do?" I asked.

"Be happy while we wait. You two go and play until Dad comes back." Mom motioned for us to run along.

"Will Dad find everything Mom said?" Conner asked, walking with me to the playground close by.

I placed my hands on my hips. "Of course he will. Mom was right before."

Conner and I played and waited for Dad's return. We came back to the camper for lunch and Dad drove up. He parked the truck, got out, and ran toward us. "Dolly, kids, I found the school, Mr. Cooper, a job, and our new home, just like Mom said."

"No, Sam, just as He said." Mom pointed to the sky.

"You're right." Dad raised his hands heavenward. "Thank you, Jesus, for all your blessings."

"When do we move into our house?" I asked.

"Praise the Lord, we can move in two days." Dad danced around with us in jubilation.

Our excitement and anticipation made two days fly by. We packed our portable tent house and said good-bye to our friends. Dad drove us to an old white two-story farmhouse. It had a ragged shake roof with black gingerbread trim. Across from the house was a large red barn with a sizable open field fenced in for "a garden in the spring," Dad pronounced.

We waited for Dad to unlock the back door. He held the door open and reached for Mom's hand. "Come on, honey." Dad smiled and leaned down to kiss her before he led her inside. "Look at this huge kitchen."

"Is the wood stove for heat?" Mom raised one eyebrow at Dad.

"Yes, but there's a gas stove to cook with." He shrugged his shoulders and walked to the adjacent living room with another wood stove. Dad pointed to a wide, cozy room north of the living room. "This is our bedroom."

"It's nice, Sam." Mom smiled and walked around.

"Let's see what's upstairs." Conner raced up the living room stairway with me and Dad close behind.

The stairway led to a spacious open play area. "This room will be Conner's," Dad announced, pointing to the south room before he turned left. "Darla, you'll get the attic room." He opened an arched door facing east.

"Wow, this room's great." I slipped under his arm and walked to the end of the room and peeked out the window.

"The sun will wake you up every morning." Dad smiled and left.

I gazed out the window at an open cornfield. What would life be like now that we were West? A loud horn blasted and we all scurried down the stairs and out the front door. The semi truck movers unloaded the remnants of our lives. They carried my boxes up to my room and I stared at the mountain before me. It was good to take one box at a time and decide to keep the treasures, give them to someone else, or throw them away. I felt clean, confident, and reorganized, eager to face my new life.

*   *   *

Sunday morning we drove to a quaint white church with a sign saying, "Welcome to the Assembly of God." I wore my red and white polka dot twirl dress under a white apron with my hair in braids tied in red ribbons. Dad escorted me to my Sunday school class in the basement. I joined eight other girls my age and we began to visit. I loved to meet people and hear their stories. In the middle of our conversation the teacher, Erma, walked in and clapped her hands to get our attention.

"Okay, girls, it's time to get started." Erma sat next to me.

I leaned over and placed my hand over her mouth. "Excuse me, but I haven't finished my story yet." Gasps filled the room and Erma's face turned red. She stood up, clasped my hand, and escorted me out of class. "Did I do something wrong?" I asked on our way upstairs.

"Yes. Where are your parents?" Erma searched the congregation from the doorway.

"Mom's in the blue dress." I pointed to her three rows from the back.

"Stay here. I'll be back," Erma said.

The church service had begun. Erma walked up to Mom seated on the aisle. She leaned down and tapped her shoulder. Mom followed Erma's finger pointing back at me.

Mom got up walked toward me. She grabbed my hand and we followed Erma into the foyer. We all stopped and they both looked at me. I knew I was in trouble. "When I tried to start class, your daughter put her hand over my mouth and told me she hadn't finished her story." Erma glanced at me. "To keep order and have time to teach the lesson, everyone needs to listen and obey."

"Darla, apologize right now." Mom wrinkled her forehead and pointed her finger at me.

"I'm sorry." I lowered my head.

"I accept your apology. I know you're excited on your first day, and the girls are too. It's okay to visit when the time's right. Today you'll have to attend the regular service with your parents. I would love to have you come back to my class next week and start over. Okay?" Erma smiled and waited for my nod before she left.

"Darla, I'm ashamed of you." Mom shook her head. "When adults talk, you have no voice. You must be quiet and listen." Mom led me into church and placed me between her and Dad. I pondered how to make up for all my wrongs. If I was perfect at home this week and made Erma happy next Sunday, it would be a good start. With a plan for home and church, I only had to worry about starting at a new school tomorrow. I prayed this time I would fit in.

I'd learned my directions and the customs of America, but I still felt peculiar and alone as the school year progressed. Girls in the fourth grade formed tight groups linked through beauty, talent, or their lifelong friends. I wasn't the image girls wanted in their group. I was small with big lips and I wore glasses—"fat-lipped four eyes," they called me. I had no common link or beauty to break into their circles. Instead I stayed in orbit, invisible, and protected from more rejection.

The next week in Sunday school I was quiet to make sure I didn't mess up my second chance. Erma asked me to share one of my life's adventures with her and the other girls after class. We each told one another something about our lives. Erma made me feel like I belonged, I mattered. Over the next few weeks Erma made extra time for me. She seemed genuinely interested in my dreams, my thoughts, and my past. Erma told me I was smart and asked me to join a girl's church group she ran.

"You want me?" I asked.

"Yes." Erma hugged me.

"I'd love to join," I blurted out and squeezed her tight. *She thinks I'm smart and she picked me. Is this a dream?*

I became part of the group and had friends to laugh, learn, and grow with every week. Part of me began to connect and yet I remained guarded except around Erma. If I didn't get too close I wouldn't feel bad when we moved again or they changed their minds about me.

My time with Erma began to include our families. Paul, Erma's husband, was quiet and gentle. A peace and security I had not felt or known surrounded him and drew me to his heart. Paul never said much, but when he did I knew I could trust him. His words and actions matched and I struggled to know how to navigate in this loving relationship. Dad was also drawn to Paul. They played baseball together on the church league, read the paper, watched sports, and took care of my brother.

Mom and Erma both joined a woman's group at church and discovered their mutual love for sewing. Over the next few weeks our family went to Erma's house during the weekends. Mom and Erma would escape to Erma's sewing room for hours. They would talk and laugh and cry. Their time together created a sister bond. In time they taught me how to stitch two pieces of fabric together to make a dress and how to connect two separate families through love. We ate, played, and shared life. I'd found my family and I felt like I belonged.

When Mom was sick, Erma would take me home with her. I helped her with their four- year-old adopted Korean daughter, Kim. I played with Kim until Paul would come and take her on an errand.

Erma always had a project for just the two of us. We would talk and laugh about her farm escapades growing up with two sisters and a little brother. She became my friend and my new angel mother.

*　　　*　　　*

Summer vacation was weeks away. To my relief I'd made it through the school year unscathed. I was ready to have a break and be home for the summer. Dad asked me to help him plant our miracle garden. We walked to the barn. He opened the door and inventoried his collection of seeds, shovels, rakes, garden hoses, and sprinklers.

"I want to show you a miracle in the waiting." Dad opened a packet of seeds and poured them into the palm of his hand. "These seed are dead. Our job is to plant, water, and weed them."

"Where's the miracle?" I asked.

"We will bury these seeds just like we buried Jesus, and God will touch them with a new life spark." Dad smiled. "In God's time they will rise out of the ground the way Jesus rose from the dead and came out of his grave. The seeds we plant are the perfect picture of Jesus and His seed in our hearts. We, too, have new life through Him."

"I want to plant miracles, Dad!" I walked with him to the garden.

"I missed the taste of yellow summer squash. I think I'll plant twenty hills," Dad said. Over the next weeks we tilled the ground, planted the seeds, watered, weeded, and waited for our miracles to come to life. As summer progressed we ate squash casserole, buttered squash, fried squash, boiled squash, spiced squash, and creamed squash as a result of planting twenty hills. We gave it to everyone and anyone we knew, and we made gourds out of what was left. I will never forget the taste of yellow squash.

Dad was right; plants are miracles and I was part of it. There's no way I could plant and harvest miracles and be all bad. I kept doing my best and looked for more miracles waiting to come to life.

The summer's heat and Mom's illnesses kept her in bed most of the time. Dad asked me to keep an eye on her in between watering the garden and playing while he was at work. I came in from the garden to check on her. I filled two glasses with cold water and pushed opened Mom's cracked bedroom door with my foot. "Mom!" I shrieked and dropped the glasses. I ran and knelt beside her lifeless body lying face down on the floor.

"Mom, Mom, wake up!" I shouted and shook her arm. "Mom, don't die," I cried. "I should have stayed by your side. I'm sorry. Conner, Conner!" I screamed.

"Darla, what's wrong?" Conner ran into the room, burst into tears, and clung to Mom.

"Mom, wake up," Conner cried and squeezed her hand. "Don't die."

"I'll call the police. Stay with Mom," I ran to the kitchen phone.

I grabbed the phone. My hand shook as I dialed the number of the police station pasted on the front of it. "Please help me," I sputtered. "My mom's lying on the floor and we can't wake her up," I cried, gasping for air.

"Take a deep breath," the dispatcher requested and I followed. "Is there another adult with you?"

"No. My dad works at Blake Elementary School nearby," I said.

"An ambulance is on the way and I will call your father," a lady's voice echoed from the phone. "Stay calm. They should arrive in two minutes."

"I need to check on Mom." I dropped the phone and ran back to Mom and Conner. Within a few minutes Dad and the ambulance arrived together. Dad gathered Conner and me in his arms and pulled us aside to let the paramedics look at Mom. "Dad, what's wrong with Mom?" I cried and clutched his arm. "Is she dead?"

Dad looked at the paramedics. They glanced at him and gave him a thumbs up. "Kids, she's not dead. Let me talk to the paramedics. I'll find out what's wrong." Dad led us to the living room couch.

We watched the paramedics roll Mom over, put a mask on her face, and poke her with several needles. She lay limp. I should have taken better care of her. What if she dies? This is all my fault.

Dad talked with the paramedics and then walked over to us. "Kids, Mom is in a coma, or a deep sleep, because the sugar in her blood's too high." Tears ran down his face.

"Is she going to heaven?" I whimpered.

"No." Dad wiped his tears and tried to smile. "She'll need to go to the hospital so the doctors can fix her."

"You kids saved her life. She'll be okay," one of the paramedics said, as several of them lifted Mom on a gurney and put her in the ambulance.

We tailed the ambulance to the hospital and sat in the waiting room to hear from the doctor. Dad took care of paperwork while Conner watched cartoons and wiggled in his chair. My eyes fixed on the TV, but the picture of Mom lying motionless on the floor kept flashing in my mind. *I should have stayed in her room and caught her. God, please let her come home. I promise I will take better care of her.* A long hour passed and the doctor came out to talk to Dad. "Your wife's critically ill with diabetes. She'll need to stay in the hospital for several weeks while we regulate her diet and medication."

Dad's eyes filled with tears. "Thank you, Doctor." Dad cleared his throat. "Can we see her?"

"Yes, two at a time. A nurse will stay with one of your children while you take the other one in to visit for a few minutes. You kids saved your Mom's life. You should be proud." The doctor patted us on the head, smiled, and walked away.

"Dad, I want to see Mom." Conner pulled at his arm. "I need to see if she's okay. I want to go. Come on, Dad."

"Darla, I need to take Conner first. You understand?" Dad waited for my head to nod yes and led Conner through the ICU doors. I buried my face in my hands and sobbed. *It's all my fault. I don't deserve to see her first.* I felt a hand on my head and I raised it to see Erma.

"Erma." I lunged into her arms and cried. "I should have stayed with Mom. I'm sorry."

"Darla, it's not your fault." Erma held me close. "Please calm down. Dolly will be all right. I will take you in to see her when your Dad and Conner come out. She'll be okay."

Within a few minutes I calmed down. I was not alone. Dad and Conner came out and Erma and I went in to see Mom. She had many tubes and wires trailing out of her connecting to various machines. She was pale and in a deep sleep. The beeps, bleeps, and the rise and fall of her chest assured me she was alive. "Mom, I'm sorry." I held her arm and sobbed while Erma rubbed my back.

"Come on, Darla, we need to go." Erma led me out to a waiting room chair while she visited with Dad. She walked back to me. "Darla, you'll come home and stay with me and your dad will take care of Conner until Dolly comes home."

Erma took me to the spare bedroom she'd set up for me six months earlier. I had stayed with her, Paul, and Kim when Mom was sick, which was often several times a month. I sat on the bed and looked up at Erma. "Erma, I thought Mom was dying," Erma sat down and held me as I sobbed in her arms. "It is all my fault. It's all my fault!" I screamed and rocked back and forth. "I'm so bad. I wish I was never born!" I shrieked uncontrollably.

"Darla, stop." Erma's hand struck my cheek. I gasped and stared at her. She gently cupped my cheeks with her hands and looked into my eyes. "I'm sorry I slapped you. You were hysterical and out of control. I had to stop the bad thoughts in your head. I love you and I can't let you think those lies." She wiped my tears. "God made you and He has a plan for you. He picked your parents and they planned and wanted to have you. Your mom's physical problems are not your fault." Erma handed me a tissue from the nightstand. "Most of your mom's problems happened before you were ever born and some of her problems were created by her bad health choices."

"What do you mean?" I blew my nose.

"When your mom was young she had to be hospitalized from the beatings she endured by her alcoholic father, your grandfather." Erma sighed. "These beatings damaged her body and her mind. During her hospitalization she received the attention she longed for from her parents and others. The damage to Dolly's body left her prone to other physical problems and illnesses. Your mom's been on the verge of diabetes for quite a long time but she's refused to follow the doctor's orders to properly take care of herself. I believe she thinks diabetes will get her the love and attention she desires. Her past experiences have blinded her to the love and attention she has here with us."

"How can Mom be so blind?" I asked.

"Her little girl heart was starved and dried out like a sponge with deep holes from the lack of healthy love and attention from her parents. We are all wounded at some point. Your mom's wounds go deep. They have a protective covering like a scab, but underneath the hurt has become an infection. To bring healing, she must be willing to open the wound and ask God to clean it out and heal it. This is a process we must go through. We can't go under, around, over, or avoid it. We must go through our pains to master them or they will master us." Erma held my hand.

"Mom loves God with all her heart and He talks to her. Why doesn't He fix her?" I asked.

"God won't take or force you to give him all the pieces of your broken heart. You have to freely surrender them all to Him," Erma said.

"Why doesn't she give them all to him?" I wrinkled my forehead.

"Your mom's too afraid and ashamed to open the painful memories and share them with God. God knows every detail of her life, but He wants her to ask Him for help and to go to Him with everything. She tries to forget her pain in her books, TV, sickness, and through her imaginary worlds." Erma pulled one leg under her. "Unfortunately, hurts won't go away by themselves. We can't truly heal without Christ's help. They grow like weeds in the dark, choking and deforming our good memories and healthy thoughts. She chooses not to face her fear or learn another way to release her pain to God. You didn't do it. You must not believe you are responsible for her illness or pain." Erma held me close and I collapsed and sobbed.

Several minutes passed and I pushed away and stared at her. "Then why does Mom say I'm a miracle, but when I was born I ripped everything out of her and she's never been the same? I hurt her." Tears streamed down my face.

"Many people have physical challenges when they give birth, and that's a risk they choose to take. Your mom's body was a mess before you were born. You are not the cause of your mom's physical problems. I know she doesn't realize how much she hurts you when she says this or she wouldn't say it. I will talk with her." Erma hugged me close until my tears ceased. "Let's get to bed. We'll visit your mom tomorrow."

Erma took me to visit Mom every day for two weeks while the doctors tried to fix her. One afternoon I was alone with Mom and I decided to ask her what diabetes was.

"It's an illness you get when you have too much sugar in your blood," Mom said.

"Did you get it from eating all your candy?" I asked.

"No, diabetes comes from your family's blood. My mother has it and my grandmother died from it." Tears ran down her cheeks. "And now I have it."

"Mom." I stroked her hand. "The doctors have medicine to fix you. Don't they?"

"I don't want diabetes," Mom sputtered. "There's no cure. It kills you a little at a time." She reached for a tissue on her table. "My grandmother's eyes failed, her heart grew weak, and her kidneys stopped. She was hooked to a machine several times a week to clean out her blood. The worst part of the disease is how it affects your immune system."

"What's an immune system?" I asked.

"Your immunity is your good body cells' ability to fight the germs and infections you get." She blew her nose. "My grandmother got infections in her legs and they didn't heal. They had to cut them off several times to keep her from dying. But she died anyway, with no legs. I don't want my legs cut off," Mom sobbed. "It's this bad Indian blood."

Instantly, I realized I had the same blood. "Will I get diabetes?" I whispered.

72

"I hope not." Mom squeezed my hand and wiped her tears. Erma walked back into the room. "It's time for you to go. I'll see you tomorrow when I come home."

"Bye, Mom." I kissed her and walked toward the door.

Erma talked to Mom for a few minutes before we left. *Maybe if I keep a better watch on Mom, she can keep her legs.*

Dad, Conner, and I brought Mom home from the hospital. She had to poke her finger several times a day to check the sugar in her blood. She had to give herself a shot in the morning and take a pill at night. Dad instructed us kids to watch if Mom ever got dizzy or sleepy for no apparent reason. If she looked weak, we were to get her a glass of juice or a piece of hard candy. I didn't understand why we needed to feed her more sugar after the doctor said she shouldn't eat it. But I decided not to ask.

Mom grew stronger each day in my care. I worked hard to make up for not being there when she got diabetes. I felt a chasm between Dad's heart and mine. He didn't request my help or seek me out to talk to anymore. I would catch Dad looking at me with sadness and frustration in his eyes, the same glance I caught from Mom on occasion. Erma told me I wasn't to blame for Mom's pain, but their frequent looks proved otherwise. Dad would mention a good deed of mine only to morph it into stabbing comments that sliced at my heart. It seemed I could never do things right or ever do enough. Dad joked and laughed with everyone but me now. Everyone thought he was the greatest dad, but for me everything had somehow changed. I believed I had to try to fix my wrongs and I endured the painful remarks waiting to hear a good one like I had in the past. The memories of the good ones kept a hope that one day they would forgive me and love me. This hope was worth it in my mind.

Chapter 11

"Family faces are magic mirrors. Looking at people who
belong to us, we see the past, present and future.
We make discoveries about ourselves."
—Gail Lumet Buckley

Mom was sick again and I stayed with Paul and Erma. I felt complete love and safety with them. Erma always had time to talk with me and tell me funny stories about her family. For years I'd tried to put our extended blood family out of my mind. Hearing Erma's stories only increased my desire to know more about my family. I was twelve and my mind demanded answers.

The opportunity to find these answers came when Erma and I were sewing. "Erma, sometimes when Mom looks at me it's as if she's afraid or sad, so she turns away. What did I do wrong?"

"You didn't do anything wrong. I believe when she looks at you she sees a reflection of herself as a little girl because you look so much alike. Your image reminds her of her past and her pain." Erma led me to a chair at the kitchen table.

"Will she ever see me or be able to love me?" I asked.

"Yes, in time." She squeezed my hand. "Right now she loves you the best she can. She's stuck in her past."

"Mom told me how the white man put our people on reservations and were mean to them." I sat up. "Is this part of her pain?"

Erma got each of us a glass of water and sat down at the table. "I think it's time you hear what your mom's life was like. Let's start at the beginning with your Grandma Dorothy, your mom's mother. She grew up in cruel and horrible times in Native American history. On the reservation the white men wouldn't allow the tribe to speak their language, perform their traditions, or practice their religion. They considered them heathens, or less than human, and treated them with cruelty. In the middle of winter, the white men gave gifts of blankets contaminated with the smallpox virus to your tribe. They had no immunity to fight the disease and tens of thousands of them died. Your Grandma Dorothy witnessed this horror with her own eyes."

"They murdered them," I whispered.

"Yes, your tribe had no one in power to fight for them. Not many white people took the time to get to know them, understand them, or respect their differences. The tribes dulled their pain through alcohol, a liquid drug, also given to them by the white man. The alcohol created terror, pain, and abuse for many generations. By the time your mom grew up on the reservation in the 1940s and 1950s, poverty, shame, guilt, anger, and abuse replaced their identity and confidence as individuals and as a tribe."

"What a terrible life. If white men were so bad to us, how come Mom married Dad?" I tilted my head.

"In her eyes, only the white world had power." Erma held my hand. "She felt like Cinderella in a fairytale when a white man, her Prince Charming, chose her and took her away from the reservation. She believed leaving her life on the reservation would free her from her pain, but we both know it didn't. Let's get back to your Grandma Dorothy. Reservation life was very hard back then. When she was only twelve, she ran away and married your Grandpa Moe." Erma sighed.

"She was thirteen years old when she had your mom."

"She's one year older than I am." I raised my eyebrows. "I can't imagine having a baby in two years or being married. Why did she do that?"

"I don't know. Your mom never said." Erma took a sip of water. "When your mom was born right after Christmas, your Grandma Dorothy placed her in a doll box near the opened wood stove to keep her warm. That's why your mom's nickname is Dolly."

"What's Mom's real name?"

"You don't know?" Erma looked surprised. "It's Elaina."

"All we've ever called her is Mom or Dolly," I said. I wondered what else Mom was hiding.

"Your grandpa and grandma were prisoners to the controlling power of alcohol. They would go to the bar and leave your mom to watch her four younger brothers and baby sister in the car for most of the day, and sometimes all night," Erma said. "Usually, they would leave your mom at home up in the canyon, nine miles from town. She would take care of her brothers and sister for days or weeks at a time without enough food. Your mom said she felt like 'a baby raising babies.'"

"This is awful, Erma," I whispered.

"Your mom was grateful for your Great Grandpa Joe and Great Grandma Elaina, your Grandma Dorothy's parents. Once they realized your mom was left with all her siblings, they would check on them. If they found the kids alone, they would take them home to care for them and love them.

"The way Zafarrah and you were there to care for me?" I asked.

"Yes," Erma said.

"Your Great Grandpa Joe was a sheriff and raised cattle to feed the tribe. Your mom was named after your Great Grandma Elaina. She helped Dolly find Jesus. She would tell your mom to run to Jesus and to her when things got bad. She did her best to protect your mom, but she couldn't stop your grandpa from hurting her." Erma's eyes watered.

"Why did Grandpa hurt Mom?" I asked.

"I will get to that in a minute. First you need to know a little more about your Grandpa Moe. He was a chef and he could get jobs when he wanted to, but most of the time he wanted to drink. Your grandpa stood six feet, six inches tall, and he could easily hold a basketball in each hand. He was mean when he drank, which was almost every day. When the alcohol mixed with his anger and his size, he was a runaway bulldozer hurting everyone in his path."

"What made him drink?" I asked.

"People drink and do drugs to escape and numb their painful past, their feelings, and their fears. These drugs make them feel a false sense of peace, power, and control, even if it's for a little while. I heard your grandpa grew up with the same family violence and drinking, so he followed this pattern instead of learning something new." Erma sighed. "Darla, I'm going to tell you what I believe has created most of your mom's pain."

"What is it?" I leaned closer.

"As your mom's physical body matured, your grandpa would bring his friends home and they would attack her and do bad things to her private parts." Erma wiped her tears. "Dolly ran when she could,

78

and when she couldn't she escaped the terror, torture, and shame by drifting to a far off place in her mind."

"Is that when her pretend spells started?" I raised my eyebrows.

"Yes, she didn't and doesn't use alcohol to escape from her painful memories; she does it all in her mind." Erma looked down.

"Why didn't Grandma stop Grandpa and his friends?" I questioned.

"Your grandma was young and she was also beaten down in her body and spirit until she felt worthless and powerless. Your grandpa and the men who hunted her and your mom were larger and stronger."

"You mean Grandpa hurt my grandma, too?" I whispered.

"Your grandma's life was a continual circle of hurts and disappointments like your mom's. She didn't want to give up the way she felt when she drank alcohol and she didn't reach out to God for help. Your mom looked to God and found a way out. When she was seventeen, she left the reservation to live with foster parents. They took care of her until she was nineteen."

"How come Mom didn't tell me about all this?" I asked.

"It's hard for her to share her past." Erma inhaled deeply. "She thinks if she doesn't talk about it, she won't hurt anymore. In her mind it's a defense. I shared all this with you in hopes you might understand your mom's life a little more and not be so angry at her." Erma held my hand. "It doesn't excuse the pain she caused you. It gives you a picture into her life so you'll see she didn't know another way to act. In fact, only through God and her foster parents did she see and learn a healthier way to parent and treat people. Dolly was able to avoid the alcohol and the physical abuse to you kids. Darla, she did the best she could at that moment in time. We're all flawed and carry hurts. With God's help we can do better with our children. She doesn't hurt you on purpose or out of anger. But she has hurt you. I pray this new knowledge and understanding will help you forgive your mom and heal your hurts. I don't want you to get stuck in the same prison of pain she's locked in."

"I don't either." I looked down.

"Remember the Bible verses where God talks about many kinds of pots?" Erma pointed to her pitcher collection on the shelves of the dining room wall.

"Yes, some are for work and some are for noble things," I replied.

"Your mom and dad have many holes in their pots, like we all do. If a pot has too many holes it can't hold water," she said. "Let's say the water's love. If it can't hold enough love for itself, how can it have any love to share?"

"Does their time and energy work the same way?" I asked.

"Yes, why do you ask?" Erma tilted her head.

"The other day I asked Mom why I was the one who always left home when she was sick or when Conner needed more attention." Tears again streamed down my cheeks. "Mom looked at me and said she and Dad only had enough energy to take care of her and Conner and I had you, so I shouldn't complain. Erma, if Conner and I were drowning and they had to pick one child to save, it wouldn't be me," I cried. "I'd be on my own. I'm Native American, bad blood in Mom's eyes. I'm not worth their time and energy. Why did God let me be born? What did I ever do to deserve this pain?"

"Darla, I'm sorry." Erma put her arm around me. "God made you a special pot and you don't deserve to be hurt. Their lack of love, time, and energy doesn't determine your value. They haven't let God help them fix all their hurt cracks and now they have turned into large holes. Now it's impossible for them to have and give you the love and attention you need. It's not something you did or didn't do. I know you're hurt and unfortunately you'll be hurt again in life. The most important thing is what you'll think and do when you get hurt again. Will you give your heart to God and let Him fix it, or will you be angry, bitter, and vengeful and create your own prison?"

"I don't want to be like them. I want a full pot," I said.

"I want that for you, too. It is a choice. I love you." Erma smiled.

"Erma, you've told me about Mom's family. What about Dad's?" I asked. "Mom said Dad has three older brothers and one younger sister."

"Your Grandma Elsie, your dad's mom, died shortly after his sister was born," Erma said.

"She did?" I said.

"Yes. Your dad was five years old. Your Grandpa Charles, his dad, sent his sister to live with two aunts who weren't married, but he kept all the boys together. He did his best but he was also mean, short-tempered, and impatient with the boys."

"Did he drink too?" I asked.

"I'm not sure." Erma shrugged her shoulders. "Your mom said he had a mean heart and words to match. Your Grandpa Charles constantly moved your dad and his brothers around until he found another lady to marry." Erma clasped my hand. "His step-mom would lock your dad in a closet all day or out of the house for several days with no food. Your dad never knew the love or gentleness of a woman until he met your mom."

"I see why they fell in love," I said.

"They love you kids the best they know how." Erma held my face. "They didn't know a healthy way to handle their emotions inside or cope with their past pain. These two factors gave them no way to deal with the hard times of raising kids, especially when there were special circumstances."

"I'm glad God gave me you." I smiled.

"Me too." Erma patted my hand. "It's a gift to have spare parents, because even the healthiest ones can't give a person all they need."

*   *   *

From the time I was eight until I was eleven, we'd moved five times and changed schools three times. The older I got, the more I longed for what my other friends had—the stability and security of a permanent home. I believed God answered my prayer when Dad announced he had bought three acres of land out in the country for us to build our dream house. We'd start building at the end of the school year. Mom had talked about her dream house for years, but I dismissed the fantasy every time we moved. Watching Dad and Mom rearrange the plans and stake out our house on the land brought this dream into reality. Dad drove out to the ranch before work every morning and laid out 2 x 4's on the floor in the shape of walls. After school in nice weather we'd ride the bus out to the ranch and meet Mom. She'd tell us where to hammer nails and help us clean up for the next day. This continued for several weeks and we slowly saw our work resemble the shape of a house. Once the walls, roof, and windows were in place, people from church completed the electric and plumbing throughout the house. Dad hired a company to hang and finish the sheetrock so we could paint it. I painted my room a solid cotton candy pink to surround my first new bedroom set, white with gold trim and a canopy bed. At last I was a princess; my dreams were coming true. I had just turned twelve when we moved in. I lay in my royal bed feeling grateful to be a part of the creations in my life through the gardening, sewing, and building of our house. I hoped our home would give me a permanent place to rest and calm the emotional swirl within our family brewing just below the surface.

Mom's dream house didn't cure her. She bounced between a variety of illnesses, more sick than well, for the next two years. I searched to find a way to be loved by her. My desperate longing began to affect my physical health. I couldn't sleep through the night; I had a constant sore throat, swollen lymph glands, and sharp stomach pains. Mom took me to the doctor and spent time with me and cared for me. I clung to Mom's attention and love. No matter how sick I became, Mom eventually got sicker, leaving me to take care of us both. The weeks of long quiet hours in bed, the time I spent caring for Mom, the schoolwork I had to make up, and the missed time with friends in church helped me realize I didn't want to be sick. It wasn't fun and there was no way to be sicker than Mom. I wanted to live.

My hope for my family's emotional tumult to calm disappeared. Mom's illnesses were plagued with constant anxiety attacks which often required a brown paper bag to neutralize them. The fact that Conner and I were going through puberty and becoming aware of and flexing of our wills didn't help Mom's conditions. We argued and fought more. Because of the size difference I always lost and got hurt.

Dad found extra jobs, which kept him away from home much of the time, because he said, "We need more money." I wondered if it was to avoid being home to deal with all of us. When Dad was home between extra jobs he would yell at us for keeping Mom upset and sick. At the release of Dad's words, the same anguish flickered in both Conner's and my eyes. We were bound by the guilt, shame, and self-loathing created by our parents' declarations that we were responsible for Mom's illnesses. We couldn't help Mom or ourselves at this age. All I could do was push my hurt inward so I wouldn't give my parent's a reason to leave me. I was told I had to understand, forgive, and keep everyone and everything all right. I took my role seriously so one day I could somehow earn their love.

*   *   *

My fourteenth birthday placed me on a new plateau with Mom. She said it was important for me to look nice and a little sexy so the man of my dreams would find me the way Dad found her. Mom bought fancy lace, sheer, and tight clothes for me to complete her mission.

"Mom, am I pretty?" I asked, donning a new lacy top.

"You're cute." She smiled at me. "I don't tell you that often, because I don't want you to get stuck up and think you're better than anyone else. God doesn't want us to be prideful."

My heart sank. I stared at the ground to fight back tears. *Mom doesn't think I'm beautiful, just cute.* I heard the voices of my friends' moms telling them how beautiful they were.

"Oh, cheer up, Darla. You have a great heart, and makeup can fix the rest." Mom's fingers slipped under my chin and tilted my face upward. "I'll show you how to wear eye shadow, mascara, and blush and dress you up in nice clothes. The boys will be interested in you. You'll see."

I hoped my new makeup mask and clothes would attract someone. If I pretended and believed it enough, maybe I would end up like Snow White and Cinderella. I learned to put my mask on and decorate my body with sheer tops and tight jeans, and I styled my hair. Mom was right; boys paid attention to me and talked to me. I no longer felt invisible, nor did I want to be. They listened to me and touched me. I saw myself wanted. I saw hope.

I was also elated to have Mom's approval and to access her love and attention. Wherever we went Mom was on the lookout for my prince. Saturday during our grocery shopping Mom told me she found the right man for me.

"His name is Cody and you'll meet him tomorrow after church," Mom said.

"Why can't I choose who to date?" I asked.

"You're only fourteen. You're not old enough or wise enough to know who's best for you." Mom stared at me. "You need to leave it to me."

I put on my short skirt and lacy white top. I took extra time on my hair and beauty mask before we headed for church. *What color of hair does he have? What does he do? Will I be pretty enough?* I waited in the foyer with Mom to meet him before church. He was six feet tall with blonde hair and handsome, but he was much older than me.

"Hello, my name is Cody." He shook my hand and smiled.

"Hi, I'm Darla." We talked a little more and sat together in church. My mind filled with hope. He could take care of me. I could escape from home and have a chance at happiness.

Our families went out for pizza and had a great time. Cody was wonderful and he liked me. We began to spend every weekend together. He would stay for supper and play games with my parents and me on Friday nights. On Saturdays and Sundays he would take me to a movie and dinner or take me for walks. He shared his love of the Beatles' music and his dreams for the future with me. Cody encouraged me to find my dreams and plan for them. Several times he gently cupped my face in his hands and kissed me with the softest velvet kisses. His tenderness awoke new physical tingles throughout my body. These sensations scared me. Cody would stop and hold me close and tell me everything was all right. He was my protector from life and my hope. I often cried after our dates with tears of joy for the hope of love in my future. He was a perfect gentleman and my first attempt at love.

One Saturday Cody called and said he had to work late so we couldn't go out. Mom and I went to the grocery store and we drove by his house, which was on the way. We saw my girlfriend Suzie's car parked out front. We both pretended we didn't see her car and kept silent. My mind raced. *I'm sure they're just talking, although, she is older and prettier than I am. But Cody wouldn't hurt me; he cares for me.*

Later in the evening Cody stopped by. "Cody, why was Suzie's car outside your house?" I asked.

"Uh, that's why I came over." Cody fidgeted. "I need to talk to you."

"Okay." I sat on the couch while he joined me.

"Darla, you are a wonderful young lady and someday you'll be a fantastic woman, but I am twenty years old and you are only fourteen." He held my hands and looked into my eyes. "I need more out of a relationship than you are ready to give, and you shouldn't be ready at your age. I'm sorry. This was a mistake." He walked out the door.

I stood up and walked to my room. I threw myself on the bed and sobbed. *If I'm wonderful, I would be enough. Clearly I'm not, again. This time I'm a mistake. God, will I ever be enough for anyone to completely love me?*

Mom came in and sat beside me on my bed and rubbed my back. "Darla, it's okay. We'll find you another man to take care of you."

"How could Cody and Suzie do this to me?" I cried.

"Sometimes things like this happen." Mom sighed. "You can't let them know how much they hurt you. You'll have to face them at church tomorrow and you need to show them you're strong by looking happy, even if you have to fake it. This is the hard part of growing up. You can't let them see you weak or down." Mom got up and left me alone.

I continually had my radio playing in my room. On cue the words, "Don't cry out loud. Remember you almost had it all," began to play from the song "Send in the Clowns." My pain and tears beat my heart numb until sleep swallowed what remained.

At church I followed Mom's advice pretending my pain away

when I saw Cody and Suzie together. I chose to appear happy despite the way I felt. My decision uncovered a sense of inner strength and defense I could use to protect myself in the future. I had an uneasy feeling I would need it.

Chapter 12

"I am not so different in my history of abandonment
from anyone else after all. We have all been split away
from the earth, each other, ourselves."
—Susan Griffin

My family's chaos continued. Ever since I met Erma and Paul when I was eight, I had lived half of my life with them. By fourteen I wanted to stay in the peace and consistency of their home, but I still longed for my parents to love and take care of me, too. When Erma said she loved me, I believed it because she'd hug me, encourage me, and take care of me with a sea of unconditional love. I didn't feel responsible to take care of her or guilty for not taking care of her. She was my new angel Mother, like Zafarrah.

My parents were unreachable emotionally and often physically no matter what I did. When I would go back home it seemed that Conner and I would end up in a fight that ended with me being hurt. *Why don't my parents protect me, the smaller younger one, the girl?* I struggled to make sense of my life and I wanted answers. I went inside to Mom's sewing room and waited for her to look at me.

"Mom, why don't you stop Conner from fighting with me?" I asked with my hands on my hips.

"You are brother and sister and you will fight. It's normal." Mom replied.

"He's bigger and stronger than I am, and I am a girl and he's a boy, so how is that okay?" I wrinkled my eyebrows.

"You need to be a woman of peace. That means you need to be more understanding and forgive him and walk away no matter what he says or does. It's your role as a woman of God," Mom said.

"But . . . ," I stammered and stomped my foot. "Why doesn't he have to be nice and understanding to me?"

"Because you are able and he's not; therefore, you must," she said.

"He could learn!" I shouted and ran to my room. *I'll bet if I was picked, or had different blood, or I hadn't hurt her she would make him be nice and understanding to me. I can't change any of that but I can be a woman of peace in hopes that someday Mom might love me. I have to believe one day she will. It's all I have.*

During the emotional roller coaster ride of Mom's and Dad's escapes and my living between two homes, my parents made a surprising announcement. They had sold our house and we would move to Kansas immediately. My heart shattered. Erma and Zafarrah flashed through my mind. My angels were ripped away, leaving me with no one to count on once again. "Why Kansas?" I asked.

"Because things are expensive in Loveland and we need to live within our means." Dad glanced at Mom who looked away. "If we live in a smaller town, we'll feel more connected and Conner will have a chance to play sports. He will have the opportunities he deserves to be great."

What about me? What will happen to me? I didn't understand and I didn't have a choice. I begged Mom and Dad to let me stay with Erma and Paul. They refused to burden them with the responsibility of me as they were adopting their fifth child soon. They also instructed me that I would be selfish to even ask Paul and Erma. I could never hurt Erma and Paul so I kept my heartbreak quiet. Erma and I spent many hours crying over our impending separation. My only comfort was the fact that we were moving to the same town where her sister lived and she would come for visits. We packed our belongings into a horse trailer and a moving truck. Paul and Dad drove them while Erma drove Mom, me, and her four children in her car. Our mini caravan headed for Kansas to start over in the middle of my freshman year of high school.

Staring out the window at the flatlands my mind was drawn to the great unknown. Life had taught me it was ever changing, unpredictable, and I was at the mercy of Dad and Mom. They were wrapped up in their ideals of Conner's greatness and somewhat oblivious to his pain and my existence. They couldn't see the pressure they placed on Conner. From the recurring strained expression on Conner's face, I'm not sure he agreed with or wanted their dreams, nor could he handle their high expectations. Many things were similar or linked between Conner and me. But my decision to keep the peace and bury my hurt after every fight and pretend everything was alright erected a wall between us growing higher and faster by the day. My reality lay in the truth that Conner had Dad and Mom and I was alone on the outside looking in.

Chapter 13

"We sail within a vast sphere, ever drifting
in uncertainty, driven from end to end."
—Blaise Pascal

Erma's sister Rebecca and her husband John let us stay with them for a few days. Dad went into town and bought a large, old two-story house that we could move into right away. We all packed in the car to see our new castle.

"It will need to be fixed up." Dad winked and smiled at Mom. Mom raised her eyebrows. "We will all get to restore a part of history," Dad said on our way into town. Conner and I viewed our new surroundings in silence in the back seat. The town was older and smaller with many farmers walking around. Dad switched our lives from the city setting of "Get Smart" to the country landscape of "Daniel Boone." We drove through town on Main Street and reached the east outskirt of town. Dad pulled into the driveway of an enormous white dilapidated two-story house in dire need of repair and paint.

He helped Mom out of the car and up three stairs. "Okay, Honey, I want you to close your eyes because this is a big house with wood floors. No peeking." Dad kissed her, opened the door, and led her inside. We followed in anticipation that we would find a great interior. The walls and ceilings were speckled in various colors and patterns of several layers of wallpaper hanging down in strips and a thick layer of dirt covering every surface. This was the worst home Dad had ever led us into.

"We can't paint until summer, but we'll do our best to make it home," Dad announced. "Won't this be great?"

"Wow, Sam, this is a big house." Mom attempted to grin.

"It's big and historic, isn't it?" Dad asked.

"Yes." Mom kissed him and walked through the house. Dad was alone in his excitement, unconscious of our shock and worry. I recognized the fake yes on Mom's face when her heart wanted to scream. Conner and I couldn't muster up the strength to pretend. This time neither one of us volunteered a bright thought to share. We didn't have one. It looked like a dump to me. Was this how life would be here? *God help me.*

We cleaned for two days and then moved our belongings inside. I helped Mom unpack and organize her twenty pairs of patterned and dyed high heel shoes and outfits to match.

"Mom, why do you keep all these clothes and shoes if you can't fit into them?" I asked.

"I guess I want to hold onto my memories and dreams." She sighed as she caressed her clothes.

"Is that why you collect pretty things?" I asked.

"I grew up poor and we didn't have money to buy anything beautiful or extra." Mom smiled. "When your dad traveled, he brought me gifts to fill my life full of beautiful things. He said it made him feel like I was with him. He's so wonderful."

After helping Mom with her bedroom we went downstairs and unpacked her eclectic world collection of knick knacks and placed them in her hutches. Other than the hutches, a dining room table, and a few other coffee tables, our living room and dining room area was bare. We'd left our living room furniture when we moved. Dad promised Mom she could pick out new furniture when we were settled. She asked Dad about going to the furniture store and he replied we couldn't afford to go because we needed to fix our house. He told her he would take care of it. Mom's eyes revealed her disappointment but she smiled and said okay.

Dad went looking for furniture early Saturday morning. He came home with dirty, worn out, wobbly furniture from the thrift store. Mom was crushed. She went from a new, custom-built house with nice furniture to an old fixer upper with tired, discarded rejects for furniture.

"Well, what do you think?" Dad asked Mom.

"This will be fine." Mom forced a grin. "I have some extra blankets to cover them." Mom did her best to make it clean. I never heard her object to Dad even though I often saw frustration and disappointment momentarily flicker in her eyes. She was using her own advice, to never let Dad see her hurt or down.

School was pleasant and enjoyable for the first time in my life. Being the new girl in my freshman class of 65 peers was exciting. I made friends easily and I was voted a homecoming attendant my sophomore year. I was grateful to be included and to feel special in some way.

School also offered me a new experience of having girlfriends to hang out with. We talked, laughed, listened to music, and I learned how to drink alcohol to fit in. Most of their moms worked, but they still found time to attend their school events and spend time with them at home. My friends would ask me why Mom was so sick. I'd tell them she had a bad case of diabetes and they left it at that. I only gave them half the truth. The other half was the fact that my parents didn't have time for me. Both truths resulted in their absence at my choir concerts and homecoming attendant celebration. Over time I quit giving them my event schedules or asking them to come to avoid more pain. I was full of excuses for my friends but not for my aching heart.

Dad had said we needed to move to a small town to be more connected, but I saw the opposite effect on Mom. Dad was gone most of the time, working at least two jobs for "more money" and left Mom alone to deal with us kids.

Mom didn't find the same friend connection at our new church she'd experienced with Erma. She was all alone and resorted to her escapes to deflect her new life. Mom stayed up half the night to watch movies and read a novel at the same time or sew in her craft room. Her night owl schedule helped her avoid facing any more of the day than necessary, leaving little time for me.

Mom also withdrew from going out of the house. She became a prisoner in her own home. I saw her read her Bible many times a day, and she would assure me all the answers I ever needed were in God's word. For all the answers she claimed to have access to, her reality was living in sickness and fear. It had been many years since she'd heard from God and I wondered why God quit speaking to her. I knew God didn't leave us, but did He get mad at us? If she was still so close to God by reading the Bible, why was she getting sicker and disappearing more?

My home life was getting harder by the day. The tension and competition between my brother and I illuminated the mean comparisons and fights my girlfriends were having. The bickering fights over who was prettier, what they wore, and whom they liked began to overshadow the happiness I experienced with them at the start. I believed I was below average so I couldn't, and therefore didn't want to compete or fight. The voyage of their relationships ebbed and flowed, but their lifelong history ties brought them back together and kept them close. No matter how much I clung to the outside to form a close friendship, I couldn't ride their waves. The disappointment and rejection added to my present pain, so I followed Mom's example and distanced myself for protection. Besides, I had enough drama at home.

Conner had a hard time making friends. His red hair, blue eyes, and porcelain complexion made girls swoon over him. The girl's reactions fueled the jealousy inside of several boys who took out their insecurities by bullying him. Their cruel treatment and rejection hurt him. His few friends were from the wealthy or socially high-positioned families. He craved their image, status, acceptance, and perceived ease of life. Their lives were the complete opposite of his and they became his inspiration. I could see the pressures of being favored and the great expectations that he must be so wonderful and successful weighed down his heart and soul. Mom and Dad had unknowingly put both of us in our own invisible prisons. We were both desperately doing everything we could to escape the pain and torment from within. My home life became a vicious cycle of shame and resentment, with rare occasional moments of attention and love.

Chapter 14

"A storm was brewing. The wind had picked up and a mass
of purple clouds was coming in from the West. It felt good
to have my hair whipping around my head. I thought it might
feel good to have hail beat down on me. Sometimes storms
outside
are the only relief for storms inside. . . ."
—Elizabeth Chandler

At the end of my sophomore year I was invited to a church youth
group that met on Wednesday nights. I looked forward to finding other
people my age who believed in God. I prayed this would change my
life. A handsome boy named Stuart struck up a conversation with me.
He shared that he planned to go to seminary to become a preacher. We
became friends and started to go steady. He shared his pain and shame
with me. He was a result of the gang rape of his mom, who was also
part Native American. We were similar in two ways: neither of our
parents had money and we both loved the Lord. I felt safe and hopeful
for love and a happy future with him. I discovered how close I could
get to another human through a kiss and touch. My emotions and
sexual desires made me long for his complete love. Over time he
began to touch me intimately.

One Friday night we were watching a movie on the couch at his
parents' house and he kissed my neck. He paused the movie and held
my hands. "Darla, I want to make love to you." Stuart gazed into my
eyes.

"I—I don't know if I can." I leaned away. "Part of me wants to, but I'm scared."

"Not tonight, but the next time we're together." Stuart turned the movie back on and put his arm around me.

I don't recall the rest of the movie. I was lost in a private conference between my mind, body, and spirit. Stuart's a Christian man who is interested in me, who wants me, all of me. *Cody was a good Christian man, but I lost him because I didn't give him enough of me to keep him. I'm scared to go all the way, scared to trust, and scared to go against God.* These thoughts continued to roll through my head for a week.

The next Friday Stuart picked me up and we went to dinner and drove around in the country until we found a vacant area of trees and parked. We began to kiss. My mind was spinning. "Well, what did you decide?" Stuart whispered in my ear. "I want to show you how much I love you and for you to show me how much you love me." Stuart caressed my cheek. "You do, don't you?"

"Yes, but . . . ," Stuart began to kiss me and unbutton my shirt. My flesh burned for him but my mind and spirit kept telling me no. I need to be loved by someone. *Maybe when he has all of me he will love me and we will be married and happy. God, I'm sorry.* In my surrender of innocence I felt no magical moment, fireworks, or profound love for me, only a jagged gash severing my heart and soul. Tears of unknown innocent sadness rolled down my cheeks. I was absorbed in a sea of grief for the shattered secret piece of me I had sacrificed and forever lost.

Over the next two months sex was the primary focus of Stuart's attention toward me. I felt my heart being cut and thrown away every time we had sex. I couldn't continue the self-torture of my spirit and soul through my body to see if he might love me. I didn't deserve this pain. I made up my mind to end our relationship. Stuart was coming to pick me up Friday night and take me out to eat. This is when I would end it.

Stuart arrived in his blue Ford pickup. I got in and took a deep breath. "Hi, Darla." He leaned over to kiss me, but I pulled away. "What's with the cold shoulder?"

"Stuart, we need to talk," I said.

"Let's talk over dinner," he replied.

"No, I need to talk with you now." Stuart turned onto a dark, dead-end street and parked.

"Okay, what's the big deal?" He turned toward me.

"I don't want to be your girlfriend anymore." I stared at him. "Stuart, I don't love you, and I won't have sex with you anymore. We're through." I reached for the door handle.

"You might be through, but I'm not," he hissed, grabbing my arm. He jerked me across the seat and pulled me out of his door with him. "You're going to give me one last screw before I get rid of you."

"No!" I screamed and thrashed to get free. Stuart locked one arm around my chest and attempted to clasp his other hand over my mouth. "Stop, please don't." I gasped for breath between his fingers that encased my mouth. He whirled me around and ripped open my shirt. "No!" I shrieked, and started to run. I felt Stuart's six-foot, 170-pound body slam my five-foot-two, 90-pound body to the ground, knocking the wind out of me.

"You better shut up, you bitch, or I'll really hurt you." Stuart straddled me and slapped my face. I kicked and punched and fought for air until his hand gripped my throat. I drifted into a place of darkness. When my eyes peeked opened I watched the taillights of Stuart's pickup disappear in the dark. I was numb. I didn't remember how I got dressed, but I instinctively headed for the safety of home.

I walked in the door and stood, numb, bewildered, and speechless. "What happened to you?" Dad asked from his easy chair while the TV continued to blare. Dad walked toward me. Mom stood up, turned away, and went upstairs to her bedroom. Dad led me into a back bedroom and closed the door. I sat in a chair by the bed, and he pulled another chair in front of me and sat down.

"Darla, what happened to you?" Dad asked.

"Stuart beat me up and," tears welled in my eyes, "he raped me." I sobbed with my face buried in my hands, longing for my dad's arms to wrap around me, to cover me, and tell me everything was going to be all right. I heard Dad's chair squeak, and I peeked up to see him lean forward and then pull back with a condemning look on his face.

"Have you had sex with him before?" Dad blurted out.

Shocked, I looked up, pushed my body backward, and stared at him. "Yes, but I told him no and to stop over and over again, but he wouldn't." I cried, holding my hands out. "He beat me and raped me, Dad."

"Well you must have done something to deserve this, to egg him on for him not to stop," Dad snapped sarcastically, and crossed his arms across his chest, barricading his heart from my pain.

I couldn't believe my own father was blaming me and telling me I deserved to be beaten and raped. My heart broke as I turned away from him and stared off in the distance, silent and paralyzed from Dad's repulsive looks and razor sharp words. Was he right? Did I deserve to constantly be hurt in my life by people who said they loved me? Would no one protect or take care of me?

"Darla, now you are damaged goods," Dad replied with a look of utter disgust. "How will you ever get a good man?"

I stood up speechless, pulverized to my core. I walked out of the bedroom and went upstairs. I locked myself in the bathroom and filled the bathtub with scalding water. I took each piece of my clothes and cut it up with the hair scissors, then threw it in the trash. I stepped into the bath to scour him off of me and wept from the depths of my soul. I sat huddled there until the water turned as cold as my heart felt. I struggled to find the energy to get out and dry off. I was shivering, so I grabbed my footy pajamas from the hook on the back of the door and went to collapse on my bed. I fell into a deep, dark pit for many days, the same one I had experienced under the staircase in Iran. But this pit was deeper, darker, and horrifying. I floated lifeless and thoughtless, yet I was riddled with pain and anguish. My mind departed my body. No light or peace was present in the pit, only downward darkness clawing at me. A scary voice from the pit called to me, pulling me farther and farther down into the core of its abyss. My mind debated whether to stay in the pit or come back toward the light and to my body. Suddenly, a brilliant ray from above illuminated my mind and transported it to my body, connecting them again. Once I was whole, the light pushed me to the surface of my life. I gasped and panted for several minutes. I felt like I'd been underwater, swimming with all my might to reach the surface before I was out of air.

"God, how could a person who says he loves me and that he believes in You rape me and throw me away like trash and never look back?" I cried and looked heavenward. "How could my own dad believe I did something to deserve this and not protect me?" I hugged Tatters. "Since I'm damaged goods, who will want me, protect me, or love me now?"

I began to hear a murmur from the dark pit. "Darla, if God loved you He would have stopped Stuart. He would have saved you. Now, look at what you have become. You can end all your pain by taking a bottle of your mom's pills."

"God, why did you let this happen to me? Where were you?" I screamed.

"God left you, and your parents have, too," the dark voice hissed.

"Stop!" I yelled, squeezing my head. "God, You said You would never leave me. How could You let this happen?" I wept into my pillow until sleep found me. I began to dream. I surveyed an enormous crowd of people who quietly held up their hands to be picked. Others jumped up and down and screamed for the teacher at the head of the room to pick them. My eyes stopped on Stuart. He looked at the teacher who was metallic on one side and dark on the other with the head of an evil man. I heard a voice from a bright light speak. "Satan must have volunteers to do his evil work by hurting others. A person's heart and master is revealed by his actions. Many choices and paths lead to painful consequences in this fallen world of sin. I was with you. I stopped Stuart from killing you. You were unconscious to spare you from more painful memories. I protected your life for the future. I will deal with him."

I awoke and realized only by God's protection was I alive. Stuart chose to do evil and I was his victim. God didn't do the evil. I still didn't understand why it happened or why Dad blamed me; I'm not sure I ever would. I struggled with all the anger of being attacked, devalued, and not defended by Dad. Inside my heart was destroyed. But I was still among the living.

When all my senses returned, I realized six meals had been placed around my room, waiting for me. I was hungry and started to eat some crunchy cheese twirls. Mom came into the room. "Darla, I'm glad to see you eating something." She sat beside me on the bed. "I've been so worried about you."

I remained silent and still. Mom placed her arm around me, and I collapsed in her arms and wept. "Darla, I'm sorry I went upstairs when you came home after Stuart raped you." I glanced at her. "When I saw you, I knew what had happened. I felt all the painful memories of my attacks," she cried. Mom and I both knew our rapist. They were supposed to be men we trusted like our dads, to defend us, but we were both wrong. "I'm sorry I couldn't be there for you," she whimpered. "Please forgive me." I had looked into Mom's eyes many times. This time I saw the same shame, guilt, and violation mirrored in mine.

"It's okay, Mom." Tears streamed down my face. "I forgive you." I embraced her until our tears passed.

"Mom, I want to go to the police. I want to make Stuart pay for hurting me."

"You can, but," Mom paused and looked downward, "you don't have any physical evidence anymore. Without evidence, it's your word against his." She placed her hand on my arm. "Because you are the new girl in town and you've had sex with him before, they will make it your fault and tell everyone you are a bad girl who sleeps around. They will hurt you more."

"Because I had sex with Stuart before, he can beat me and rape me and I have no right to fight back?" I ranted and stood up.

"Haven't you had enough pain?" Mom pleaded and looked up at me. "God will deal with him. He says vengeance is His alone. That's the way it is for you and me."

"That's not the way I want my life to be." I stormed out of the room.

God did say this, but I can't believe no one will defend me and it's wrong for me to defend myself or make someone pay for their crime. How can I ever feel safe or be happy again? Will I always feel vulnerable, fragile, and on my own?

Weeks passed and my family disregarded my rape. They never spoke of it again. I decided I would never win a court battle, so why bother? I couldn't pretend or hide from the disgust in Dad's eyes, so I avoided him at all cost. Anger and avoidance became my way to handle my anguish, but it didn't stop my pain. I tried drowning my torture in an amber-colored bottle. I spent many nights with my girlfriends, and I became the life of the parties. At first I never had a hangover; over time the hangovers arrived and then grew worse. The story Erma told me of my Grandpa Moe and Grandma Dorothy came to mind. Alcohol ruined their lives. I have enough pain in my heart and spirit. Why add more physical pain and shame? A few people asked me if I wanted to try drugs. I refused to lose control of my mind and leave myself at the mercy of boys again. Too many circumstances and situations in my life had already left me with no control. I wasn't going to volunteer for more of the same.

By the time I was a junior and sixteen years old, I worked at three jobs to pay for my contacts, class ring, and all my clothes. I realized I could take care of myself financially. I avoided church and all those hypocrites like Stuart. All I needed was God, and He was the only one I could trust or count on. This mind-set crumbled with the realities of seeing other girls in love and good boys taking care of them. My heart longed to find love, but it was consumed with fear of being hurt again. The battle inside subsided as other boys expressed interest in me. I sensed a new power when I flirted and discovered an odd control over boys when sex was the lure. I could have someone close or pay attention to me whenever I wanted. Though I felt physical sexual pleasure, I couldn't connect it with my heart. A dark voice would tell me, "You deserve to be desired and loved, to feel special and good, so enjoy yourself." This voice and my new self-power became the rationale to use sex to make me feel good. Besides, I could only lose my virginity once and since I'm "used goods," I had nothing to lose. At least with sex I could stay in control of my body and heart.

However, with each encounter my heart and spirit wrenched. One evening my heart and spirit collided. "No matter how much I try to fill my heart void with sex, I'm still empty inside," I sobbed. "God, how can I stop the hurt and shame in my heart? My soul feels vacant and lost. God help me." I fell to my knees and sobbed. The vision of Stuart, wrapped in evil, raping me, flashed in my mind.

"You were made by Me. I am here. Do not get absorbed in sin, which leads to evil and a road of death." A still voice in my spirit stopped the dark voice in my head.

"Lord, forgive me for choosing to constantly sin. Heal my heart and stop the pain." I sobbed and found a deep relief and peace.

Chapter 15

"In each family a story is playing itself out, and
each family's story embodies its hope and despair."
—Auguste Napier

To avoid the temptation of sex and alcohol, I spent more time at home. I remained in my room to avoid Dad or Conner. I couldn't handle any more fights.

I thought everything was okay until one Saturday afternoon. Dad asked me to sit down and talk with him on the couch. These talks never turned out happy so I braced my heart for the next hammer stroke to my heart. He said he had made arrangements for me to stay with Carol and Marvin, Erma's sister and her husband. "Your Mom and I only have enough energy to deal with Conner. Without you here there won't be any more fighting which is best for all of us. Besides Conner will be leaving soon to go to school. You understand don't you?" Dad's agonizing words echoed from the past, slicing open the scars in my heart.

"When do I leave?" I asked.

"I'll drop you off in a few hours. It will only be for a little while. You'll be back home before you know it," Dad said.

I turned to go to my room and pack. *I wish Erma had taken me. I wish she were here.* People claimed to love me, but they hurt me and threw me away whenever I was inconvenient. I was on my own again. This time no one came to comfort me or to give reasons or excuses why they wouldn't save me. Instead anger, resentment, and pain began to percolate in my heart.

I stayed with Carol and Marvin for two months, keeping myself detached since this was only temporary, until Conner left for school.

After Conner left for school I returned home to pretend I was loved and grateful, even if it was for a short time. I hung out with my girlfriends as much as I could and worked odd jobs to support myself and save for my uncertain future.

Chapter 16

"A person does not have to be behind bars to be a prisoner.
People can be prisoners of their own concepts and ideas.
They can be slaves to their own selves."

—Maharaji

Dad disappeared in his numerous jobs while Mom cried and disappeared in her mind. I couldn't make them interested in me or my life. I was all alone again. The more my parents withdrew from me, the more urgently I searched for a man to love me.

I waited at an intersection for a ride to school with a friend. A blond boy with a deep voice stopped his car and volunteered to give me a ride, but I declined. Our short meeting sparked my interest. I asked around and learned Mark was a bad boy with a fast car. He worked at a gas station and came from a family who was respected in the community. Mark and I ended up having study hall together and we began to talk and flirt. Mark listened to me and made me laugh. We started dating and he took me to parties. We had fun.

While Mark worked, I'd often spend time with his mother, Nina. She welcomed the company since Mark's dad, Arthur, was gone most of the week. Nina taught me how to cook a variety of meals and we became friends. It was nice to have another mother figure who liked to have me around. I was grateful for this blessing, and I relished my time with them. Finding a family to love me and fit into was a dream come true.

Mark often told me I was his ray of sunshine because I always found something to be happy about. He said I was different because I wasn't hung up on how much money he spent on me, and I would ride along with him when he went hunting. It felt great to have someone appreciate me and I wanted to be at his side constantly. This time I was determined to do whatever I needed to do to make him happy. If I got lucky, he might love me.

Mark's mom was 42 when he was born in 1962. His brother was fifteen years older and his sister nineteen years older than he. His dad was kind and good to me. I was told, however, that in his younger years he had a temper when he drank. Mark resented Arthur being gone and he always held a hidden tension for his dad. When Arthur was home, Mark idolized him one minute and tore him down the next behind his back. Arthur loved Mark and did his best to be there for him, but Mark couldn't see this. I would have traded my dad for his any day.

In Mark's eyes Nina could do no wrong and he knew she felt the same way about him. Mark had all the necessities of life, but he wasn't content or at peace. Nina constantly compared Mark to his older brother when she wanted him to change his mind or actions. Mark would get mad. But ultimately he would do what she wanted. As a result he grew angry at his brother and harbored a big chip on his shoulder.

Mark grew up in a Lutheran church and he believed in God, so he was good. He didn't see the need to be a "religious freak," and he would tease me when I spoke of God. I avoided church and the hypocrites there at this point in my life. I thought if God was in my heart, that was the most important thing.

Mark's parents never kissed, held hands, or hugged like I'd seen my parents constantly do. They were complete opposites. My yearning to feel loved and share my affections hit a wall of resistance around Mark, especially in public. "Mark, why don't you hug me or hold my hand more?" I asked.

"We don't need to crawl all over each other in front of everyone." He glared at me. "You have my ring and you're my girl and that's enough."

"You're right. I'm your girl." I smiled. Mark picked me and if he doesn't want to touch me very much, I can live with that if there's a chance he could love me.

Another contrast between our parents appeared in time. Mark's parents occasionally argued in their room when they thought no one was around or would hear them. I never heard my parents argue or raise their voices at one another. Mark said this was normal and my parents weren't normal. This was a fact I couldn't dispute. He said everyone needs to have a good fight once in a while so they can make up. Mark's parents would come out of their bedroom after yelling at one another, smiling and asking us if we wanted to play cards. Their unity proved Mark was right. This was different from my family, who dealt with anger by hiding and pretending. Maybe if my parents argued and fought, they could fix things and my life would be different.

When we had gone steady for about three months, Mark insisted it was his job to take care of me. He drove me to and from school every day and asked me about my day. His questions became more specific over time. He'd ask me who I talked to and what we talked about. It felt so wonderful to share my life. I was grateful to have someone who cared about me. Mark bristled when he saw me talking to another male in school and I felt special. Mark said he was the only guy I needed to talk to. He was my man and I was his girl, but I still wanted to talk to my guy friends.

As our relationship continued, I experienced hidden anger boiling below Mark's surface. His care and questions about my day became an interrogation. He would give me permission to do things or to speak to people and his control didn't feel right.

"Mark, why can you talk to your friends that are girls, but you won't let me to talk to my guy friends?" I asked him as we pulled into my driveway. "That's not fair."

"You're being too touchy. If I could trust you to be faithful, I wouldn't have to watch your every step." Mark gripped my face in his hands.

"I've never been unfaithful to you." I pulled away.

"I'm trying to protect you and keep you safe." He grabbed my arm and glared at me.

"Stop it. You're hurting me!" I shouted and pulled away.

"Darla, I'm sorry." He rubbed my arm. "Don't you want me to protect you?"

"Yes." Tears filled the corners of my eyes. "I'm sorry I questioned you. Please forgive me." I took his hands in mine.

"Of course I will. You're my woman. Just don't be a bitch." He pulled me close for an embrace and long kiss. His words stung deep. The last boy who called me that raped me. What was I doing wrong? Tears rolled down my cheeks. No man had fought for me or wanted to, not even Dad. He said he was only trying to protect me because he loved me. This was my dream come true.

I thought Mark gave me the love I craved, but it included explosive arguments involving him punching something or shoving me lightly. Fighting and making up became our normal routine. This cycle left me uneasy, but what could a damaged girl expect? I was blessed to have this chance, said the self-talk in my twisted Cinderella mind.

One summer evening we pulled into Mark's parent's garage and parked. Mark turned to me and placed his hands on mine. "Darla, I want to ask you a question."

"Yes, what is it?" I stared at him. Could this be real? Could he love me and want me? What if he doesn't?

"Will," Mark hesitated and reached one hand in his shirt pocket. "Will you marry me?" He pulled a ring box out and opened it toward me.

"Oh, yes." I hugged and kissed him.

"I wanted to ask you before your senior year, because I want everyone to know you are mine." He smiled.

"Yes, I'm all yours." I leaned into his embrace, ecstatic to know what it was like to be chosen.

Mark went to a technical School in Goodland during my senior year. He came home every other weekend. Our relationship bounced from happy times to explosive fights to making up. Deep in my heart uneasiness grew, but I still felt lucky to have anyone want me.

We made it through the year and I prepared to graduate from high school. While my friends' parents planned parties, acknowledgments, and rewards for their graduations, Mom was sick in bed and Dad had to work. My heart longed for their attendance to my graduation. At my graduation as I stepped onto the stage to receive my diploma, my eyes searched the audience for my parents. They were not there. I smiled and stuffed the disappointment once again. My friends asked me to come to their parties, but I lied and said my parents had a surprise waiting for me. Shame and hurt overwhelmed me. I returned my rented gown, drove home, and went to my room to escape in my music.

My dream of being a stewardess, flying to faraway places, and living in the city flashed through my mind. It was squashed by the reality that my stature didn't meet their size requirements. College was out of the question because I didn't think I could compete with the smarter and more beautiful girls. I'd just fail again. My last chance at success was to marry Mark and be a good wife and have children. Children were the only hope of anything good coming from my heart and body. This would be my destiny.

Chapter 17

"To what will you look for help if you will not look to
that which is stronger than yourself?"
—C. S. Lewis

My wedding day was set for three days after my eighteenth birthday. It would be small and simple. Erma and Mom altered Mom's wedding dress and made the bridesmaids' dresses. Together we made silk flower arrangements and Erma made the cakes. Dad was still upset because the wedding cost him $400.

Mark's angry heart occasionally brought doubts to my mind, but I convinced myself Mark would change and heal once he was with me. My dreams of a husband, children, and happily ever after were on the horizon, and no one would take this from me.

The flowers were in place, the church was full, and I was in the bridal room ready to walk down the aisle. Tears spilled under my veil. My heart began to question my mind. *Should I marry Mark? No one else wants me. This may be my only chance at love and a new start at life.* I took a deep breath and wiped away my tears. Dad led me down the aisle to Mark and I said, "I do."

Our wedding reception ended and we started on our two-hour drive to the Home Inn at Kearney, Nebraska.

"Wow, I'm sure glad that's over with." Mark adjusted his seatbelt. "All those people and that fuss."

"Wasn't it a nice wedding?" I smiled.

"I'm glad I came to Milford two weeks ago and found a house for us to rent," Mark said. "My new job's my priority now."

"You'll do great." I grinned and squeezed his hand. Mark pulled into the hotel entrance and parked. "Are we staying in the honeymoon suite?" I asked tentatively.

"No, we can't afford to waste the money since we're only here one night." Mark frowned and unloaded our suitcases, handing me mine. "Someday we can take a honeymoon, but I have to be at my new job on Monday and that's the most important thing. You understand, don't you?"

"Of course." I smiled. "We have each other and a new life, and that's the most important thing."

We checked in and lugged our suitcases to the room. Mark opened the door and carried his bag in. "Aren't you going to come in?" Mark flung the suitcase on the extra bed and headed to the bathroom.

"Yes." I walked through the door and put my suitcase beside his. The images of Dad opening the door for Mom to all the homes we lived in flashed in my head. Mark was waiting to surprise me and carry me over the threshold of our first house. He couldn't carry me now because he had to use the restroom, I reasoned.

Mark came out of the bathroom, and I went to change into my special nightgown and surprise him. A few minutes later I walked out and over to him.

"Wow, you look nice." Mark pulled back the covers. I got in bed and we kissed. "I would like to, but I'm too tired." He yawned.

"That's funny. Me too." I kissed him and rolled over. Is this how my life will be? Tears streamed down my cheeks. It's just one night and tomorrow we'll start our new life. I'm married and I need to be grateful. I silently dried my eyes and drifted off to sleep.

Morning came and we ate the hotel's free continental breakfast, loaded our suitcases in the car, and headed for our new home. "We're going to be so happy." I hummed to a tune on the radio in our car. Mark grinned and drove into town to a quaint little white shake-sided house with black shutters and parked. "It's so cute," I enthused.

"It's small, but we'll get a bigger house when we have more money," Mark said.

"Oh, it's perfect for us. Can we go in?" I grinned ear to ear with one hand on his and the other on the door handle.

"Sure, let's go." We walked hand in hand to the front door. He unlocked the door and walked in but I stopped, hoping he would carry me across this threshold.

"Darla, where are you? I thought you wanted to see the house." He walked back to the door and gave me a puzzled look.

"I was just waiting for you to carry me across the threshold because this is our first home," I remarked.

"Don't be silly. That's only in the movies. Now do you want to see the house or start moving stuff in from the car?" he asked.

"I want to see our house." I walked through the doorway alone. Our small, empty house only took a few minutes to tour. The daisy yellow kitchen and dining room stopped me in my tracks. Sunlight from the large windows that covered the south wall glimmered throughout the room. It was the happiest kitchen I'd ever seen. By the time I circled back to the front door Mark had a load of clothes in his hands. "The house is your job to take care of and I will earn a living and support us. Now help me unload the car." Mark walked into the bedroom.

We unpacked all the bags and boxes in our car and waited for the moving truck to deliver our furniture. The truck arrived and we finished just in time to fall into bed from happy exhaustion.

Monday morning I jumped out of bed and cooked my first meal for my husband before I sent him off to work. The sunshine in my bright, happy kitchen surrounded me in my chair. All my life's worries and fears evaporated into contentment with each delicious breath of the coffee encased in my hands. "Lord, thank you for helping me make my future so bright," my heart whispered.

A fresh freedom, excitement, and anticipation for my future arose inside with each box I unpacked and put away. It was my decision where to place things in my house. For once I was in charge of my life, and that felt good.

The ability to set up our home and take care of my husband also created a gush of love I wanted to share. I began to kiss the back of Mark's neck while he watched TV Saturday morning. He whirled around and grabbed my hands. "Stop acting like a bitch in heat and act like a married woman." He jumped up and pushed me aside as he stormed out of the house.

What just happened? My heart overflowed with love and I kissed him. How did I act like a dog in heat? "God, what did I do wrong? It's only a week after our marriage?" I cried. *Mark's right; life's not like the movies. Maybe he doesn't feel like a man when I come on too strong. I'm sure that's it. They say every marriage is different and I guess this is the way mine is so I will adjust and be happy.*

*   *   *

As the weeks passed, we settled into a routine. Taking care of my home and Mark made me look forward to a baby someday. One evening during dinner, Mark told me we were invited to a party on Saturday at John and Carmen's house.

"Who's John?" I asked.

"He works for the city and he and his wife are new in town, too," Mark explained as he finished his hamburger.

"What can we bring?" I asked.

"You can make brownies and I'll get a case of beer." Mark stood up and walked to his recliner in the living room, turning on the TV as he slumped in the chair.

I picked up the dishes and put them in the sink to wash. *That's a lot of beer. I'm sure Mark won't drink too much and lose his temper with his new job. Things are different now, but I would feel better if he never drank again.* I finished the dishes and joined Mark in the living room.

Saturday came and I was excited to meet new friends. Carmen greeted us at the door with a warm smile. "Hi. You must be Mark and Darla." She motioned for us to come in. "Mark, you can join the guys out back through the patio door." She pointed to the right.

Carmen guided me into the kitchen. Two other women were making hamburgers and Carmen poured me a drink. The night pressed on, and we laughed and had fun until Mark switched from beer to whiskey. He became agitated and loud and I knew it was time to go. I managed to talk him into going home around midnight. I helped him to the car.

"Darla, you're so ugly and fat. You're lucky I married you," Mark slurred on the ride home. His words left me speechless. But their sting cut a slice in my heart. I parked the car and helped him to the house. He stumbled in the door and reached for a chair to steady himself.

"I'm not ugly or fat, and if you don't want to be married to me, then don't do me any favors." I slammed the front door shut and walked to the kitchen for a drink of water. Mark stumbled through the kitchen to the back porch without a word. I slumped to my knees at the sink base and sobbed.

Suddenly my bicep seared with pain as Mark jerked me up, poking the steel of a double-barrel shotgun against my jaw. "You bitch, if you yell at me again or if you ever try to leave, I will kill you." Mark's eyes were clear and his slur was gone. He meant this. "You're my property. You better be grateful I married you after you were raped. If you weren't such a slutty, stupid, used Indian I felt sorry for, I wouldn't have rescued you from your pitiful life," he hissed. His venomous words, scented with beer and whiskey, spewed in my face. "Come on, let's go to bed." He lowered the gun and grinned while he pulled me to the bedroom and threw me on the bed.

My world exploded, my heart shattered, and my spirit froze instantly. Oh, God help me, my heart and mind pleaded quietly. Luckily, Mark was only capable of sleep. I clung desperately to the edge of the bed and my world. Why can't someone love me, my mind questioned for hours. Around 3:00 a.m. panic gripped my heart. Mark was snoring and this was my chance to call for help. I slipped out of bed and tiptoed to the kitchen, pulling the phone as close to the back door as possible. I quietly called home.

"Mom, Dad, I know it's late, but I need your help," I cried. I pressed my hand over my mouth to stifle the noise of my voice.

"Darla, what's wrong?" Mom asked.

"Mark held a shotgun to my head and," I gasped for air to keep calm, "he said if I ever left him, he would kill me." I stared at the door to watch for Mark. "Please come and get me," I begged.

"Darla, your dad needs to talk to you." Mom's voice was replaced by Dad's.

"Darla, I heard what happened, but you've made a vow to God and you chose to marry Mark, so you'll have to live with it." The phone went dead.

All the memories of devastation and abandonment by my parents exploded in my mind. *There's no one to save me. God, I can't believe they don't care.* I hung up the phone and collapsed in a heap, sobbing quietly. *How could they let their daughter stay with someone who held a gun to her head? How? My parents have never rescued me in the past; why did I ever think they would rescue me now? I'm so stupid. They don't believe I'm worth saving, and that's just my reality. Erma and Paul have six kids to raise now, so I can't call them. I'm all alone with a husband who says he loves me one minute and threatens to kill me the next. I have no way out except death. When I have children, I will never refuse to help them, never.* "God, how could it be your will for me to be hurt?" I dragged the phone back to the counter. *No matter what happens I will make it good to show them I can be loved.*

"God, I'm stuck so You must have put me here to help Mark. That must be it." I wiped the tears from my face. "Help me be a light for Mark and do whatever I need to do to please You and help him change," I prayed as I snuck back to the bed.

In the morning I awoke to find Mark gone and the shotgun locked away. He came home for lunch as usual and acted like last night never happened. Bringing up the past wouldn't change things, so I pretended, too.

The next few months Mark limited himself to two beers when he drank. This amount mellowed him, but I was ever watchful for his anger to return. We continued our daily routine and the months marched on with only sharp, critical words.

I avoided any phone contact with my parents to escape more pain. We rarely saw each other in person anyway, because their presence made Mark angry. Mark wanted me to focus on him and our life. He said he loved me and my parents didn't because they were never there for me and hurt me all the time. It was hard to disagree. Mark was the happiest when he had me all to himself. His happiness encouraged me to stay angry and away from my parents.

Chapter 18

"Love recognizes no barriers. It jumps hurdles, leaps fences,
penetrates walls to arrive at its destination full of hope."
—Maya Angelou

Three months into our marriage I began to have severe cramping and pain. I went to see an obstetrician and discovered I needed surgery to remove adhesions created by a condition called endometriosis. The doctor explained that after surgery I had a ten percent chance of ever conceiving and then only if I underwent fertility treatments right away.

Children were my only hope to find and receive unconditional love. I couldn't bear the thought of not being able to have children. For the next two years I endured many painful procedures and therapies until the joy of life welled inside my belly. Carrying my baby brought a constant, pure love in my heart and soul. It was a divine, supernatural connection I had never known. My baby completed me. The baby moved for a week, and then there was silence. After fourteen weeks I started bleeding and lost our first son. My heart shattered. Was I being punished? If I had done everything right in my pregnancy why did God take him to heaven? The loss of my son cut me to the core. I couldn't explain my life connection or my failure; I just knew a part of me was forever gone and only God could heal my deep loss. All my self-loathing and pain intensified with Mark's blame. My only belief and defense was that God knew best. I prayed for God to give me another chance and let me give Mark a son so he would love me.

It took all my faith to see the good in my pain. After several weeks I found the good; despite my ten percent odds, I could conceive. My hope was rekindled. Five months later, I welcomed twenty-four hours of "morning" sickness with open arms.

I took excellent care of myself, determined to carry this child to term and be a good mother. Peace and joy flooded my soul, despite the increasing alienation from Mark. At every opportunity, he reminded me pregnant women were fat and ugly and a turnoff. We still slept in the same bed and had sex when he demanded it, but it was all mechanical to me. Mark separated himself from us as my tummy grew bigger. I didn't care because I was carrying a miracle of pure love. At night I would sing and pat my tummy, grateful for the fourteenth week to pass. "My baby, you are loved. God has blessed us with each other. I have never felt so loved, complete, at peace, and joyful in my life," I whispered through my grateful tears.

The baby's arrival was seven days overdue, so my doctor arranged to induce labor the next morning. We arrived at the hospital at 6 a.m. and he started the inducing process. Mark was supportive at the start, but with each passing hour he grew impatient. He paced the floor, sighing and complaining how long this was taking. The baby decided to take its time and I was exhausted. The nurses asked him to be positive several times but had no success in cajoling him. Finally they threatened to remove him and he became more compliant. Once again strangers were the ones who helped me.

At 7:08 p.m. Michael arrived healthy, weighing 8 pounds, 9 ounces. The nurses cleaned him and placed a miracle of God in my arms. A rush of love flooded my soul and I covered his precious little face with my tears of joy.

"Michael, I have loved you before you were ever made and I'll love you forever more," I whispered to him as I held him. "Nothing can ever separate my love from you."

"Darla, he's beautiful." Mark took him from me and proudly announced his arrival to everyone.

"Lord, let this be a glimpse of the kind of dad he will be. Even if he's mean to me, it's okay as long as he's a great dad to Michael," I whispered to God.

The next day I reflected on Michael's birth. "God, thank You for giving me the most miraculous, supernatural experience of creating a new life. Help me to raise Your purest creation of love so his life is filled with more love than mine. God, I'm amazed how You took away all the birthing pain once I held Michael." Maybe all the pain in my marriage will lead to pure love and joy like Michael's birth. "God, You've placed me in this marriage. Help me, no matter what I have to do."

Mark took a few days off when we brought Michael home, but he refused to let anyone help me or to care for the baby himself. He repeated that his job was to earn a living and mine was to take care of him, the house, and the kids. Michael was my sole responsibility and I welcomed my bundle of love. He only cried when he was hungry or had a wet diaper. From the time he was six weeks old he slept eight hours through the night. He was the joy of my life and I loved him so.

Mark grew more angry and jealous of the time I spent caring for Michael, but he refused to let anyone else give me a break. He drank more, and he began to stay out all night from time to time. The smell of perfume followed him when he returned home, but I was consumed and exhausted with childcare and I didn't confront him. My focus was on my recovery and taking care of Michael. I did my best not to question Mark and set off his anger in my defenseless position. I was a new mom stuck in my marriage and I had to make it work somehow.

By the time he was two weeks old, Michael was having a reaction to his formula. He cried for several hours before I managed to get him to go to sleep in his swing. Mark agreed to watch him while I ran to the store for different formula the doctor had advised. I hurried through the store, but when I returned to the house and opened the front door, Mark was shaking Michael! I dropped the grocery bag and ran to Michael, swooping him into my arms. "If you ever hurt him again, I'll leave!" I yelled.

Mark grasped my arm. "I'll kill both of you if you ever try."

Keeping myself between my son and Mark was the only way I could protect him. Mark rarely helped with Michael, so that made it easy at this stage. The weeks turned into months and Michael passed his first birthday. I began to feel the familiar queasiness of morning sickness. This child's creation was a wonderful surprise, considering all the treatments it took to conceive Michael.

I felt honored to have another opportunity to carry a miracle and feel this life inside of me. Being a mother made my life worth living. The responsibilities of taking care of Michael on my own and the physical realities of pregnancy depleted all my energy and strength. I ignored Mark's detachment and unfaithfulness; I bounced between feeling trapped and grateful to have my children. All I could do was pray for God to change his heart.

Seven days after the due date, around three in the afternoon, my contractions started. I woke Mark at 3:00 a.m. and told him something was wrong and we need to go to the hospital. He called a friend to watch Michael, grabbed the bags, and we started our 45-minute drive. Mark drove like a madman, and we made it to hospital in 25 minutes.

After my initial examination, the doctor told us the umbilical cord was wrapped around the baby's neck and the baby was sideways. Any pushing could kill our child. He worked with me on every fourth contraction to see if we could turn the baby. Mark retreated to a corner of the room while the nurses and Dr. Jones tended to my every need. Sixteen hours from the first contraction, the baby turned. I was ecstatic but exhausted. "Dr. Jones, I can't do this anymore. Let's do a C-section," I cried.

"Darla, you're almost there. You can do this. Trust me." Dr. Jones looked into my tear-filled eyes.

"Ok, I can finish." I gave the last of my energy to push. Joseph was born at 7:08 a.m. and weighed 7 pounds, 3 ounces. He and Michael were both eight days overdue, and even though they were separated by twenty-one months, their birth times were exactly twelve hours apart. They were bonded by blood and in time, forever connected to my heart.

Joseph was a brilliant blue so the nurses cleaned him quickly while a pediatrician checked his vitals. Dr. Jones placed him in my arms. "Darla, here's your beautiful baby boy."

"Joseph, you are beautiful and loved." My heart overflowed with joy, showering him with my tears. "You are a miracle."

"Darla, we hate to cut your time short, but we have to get Joseph in the incubator to ensure he has oxygen to recover." The nurse placed him in the incubator next to me. I wanted so desperately to hold him, but all I could do was love him through the glass. Our separation reminded me of the invisible mental barrier between Mom and me. I was determined to surround him with love so he would never feel that pain.

We brought Joseph home, and once again I had no help. I was exhausted but thankfully God had given me another wonderful, easygoing son. Mark kept his distance, with an occasional harsh word or thump to me or Michael. I had my boys and that's all that mattered. Secretly I wished he would just disappear.

Mark came home one day from work and announced he had been transferred to Wyoming. He declared this was our chance to make a life for ourselves away from our families. We didn't have much to do with them now because Mark wanted to do things his own way. He always found an excuse to stop my parents from coming to see us or to prevent us from going to visit them. His parents rarely came because of their health issues. I already felt isolated and now we would be nine hours away from our families instead of three. Once Mark made a decision, we had no choice but to obey. In the middle of winter we packed our house, three-month-old Joseph and two-year-old Michael, and moved to Wyoming. The move was exhausting mentally and physically, but I was left to sort out the entire upheaval on my own. The cold winter and desolate area amplified my feelings of isolation. I grew more afraid.

Chapter 19

"Determination gives you the resolve to keep going
in spite of the roadblocks that lay before you."
—Denis Waitley

I loved the boys and played with them, trying my best to keep them away from Mark. All my hopes and prayers for Mark to learn to control himself and show us how much he truly loved us were disintegrating.

My vows to God, Dad's scripture quotes, and the church's message from the pulpit commanding wifely submission left me physically, emotionally, and spiritually tethered to this volcano. I struggled with the thought that this was the way God wanted it, but I didn't see another way out. My only choice was to try harder, because I refused to quit or mentally disappear from my sons.

Mark pushed, shoved, and slapped me more now, but at least he didn't beat me like an abused woman, I rationalized. He was just angry, especially when he drank. Mark never physically hurt me in front of the boys, but he continually pointed out my flaws and shortcomings in their presence. I did my best to protect them so he wouldn't get angry, without success. The only value I saw in myself was in my role as their mom.

I did everything I could to prove my value to Mark so he would love me and treat me right, but nothing worked. Mark made it clear I was a failure as a wife. He was in a pattern of blowing up, being nice, becoming frustrated, and then blowing up again. At least there were times when he was okay, and even moments when he showed some love. I was grateful for the drops of goodness and prayed somehow they would multiply.

My heart and spirit continued to wrestle with the hurt and the conflict with my commitment to God in my marriage. I read dozens of self-help and spiritual books searching helplessly to find any answers. There had to be a way to fix myself and Mark so we could finally be happy. But what was it?

I read that my power was in the thoughts I sent into the universe. Whatever I spoke would happen, if I just believed. If I gave good karma, I would get it back. One afternoon while praying I began to see all these books had one thing in common. All their power came from "I," "me," and "my" thoughts and will power, which I had been using. No matter how much I wished or hoped, confessed or willed myself to change and be a better wife, it hadn't worked. I'd been doing what the books said without positive results. Deep inside, my spirit questioned the suggestions from other people and religions to keep my imperfect self as my ultimate wisdom and authority. All one afternoon, my core kept whispering something wasn't right.

"God, I'm not the creator of the universe. You are. Forgive me for making myself my own god or trying to find a false one. Help me put You at the center and trust You alone," I prayed that night.

I knew I had to get back to church and have a deeper relationship with Christ. There had to be someone there who could help and support me. They couldn't all be bad. The boys and I began to attend church and Sunday school regularly. I read Bible stories to them just like Mom had to me, hoping they would see God as good and loving.

For all of my parents' faults I was blessed from an early age to see and know God through them; I prayed my boys would see God in me. During my spiritual reawakening, God's word came alive in my heart and spirit as I read the books of John, Hebrews, Peter, and James. I realized I'd used God when it was convenient for me, but most of the time I kept Him on a shelf. Still God had never left me. God helped me see myself as a new creature and any good in me was a result of Christ in me. I wanted to share my revelations with Mark, but he refused to talk about God. My beliefs only ignited his anger.

My change of mind and heart in Christ brought more questions about my marriage, but I wasn't sure I could risk making God mad at me if I broke my marriage vows and left Mark. Through all my studying I realized that in the past my obedience equaled approval and value by others. I had tried so hard to be a good mother, and yet how could I keep my boys safe while staying married? One way to protect them was to never let them see me down or hurt. I couldn't leave Mark or he would kill us all. "Somehow, God, help me make this work," I pleaded.

Mark's physical abuse increased toward the boys, and I began to fear for our safety more and more. He grew more irrational, unpredictable, and full of rage. To everyone on the outside we were a nice little family. On the inside we were battered and breaking apart with each passing day.

My relationship with Christ gave me compassion and helped me forgive the past hurt my parents had inflicted. Mom and I secretly shared our hearts several times over the phone, and I found hope that one day we would have a good relationship. Mark was oblivious to my heart change with Mom. He continued to find excuses to keep them away, but I persisted for the boys' sakes.

Mark finally agreed to let my parents come for a visit and watch one of Michael's T-ball games. We all went to the ball field and waited for Mark to join us after work. He never showed up for the game or returned home the entire night. The next day we played with the boys and did our best to make life happy, trying to hide the fact Mark wasn't there. Mark slithered in drunk at 3:00 a.m. He yelled and punched a hole in the bedroom wall. I tried to pacify him and keep the boys from hearing his rage before he passed out. Mom and Dad had to hear him from the guest room next to ours, but no one came to my rescue. To my relief, Mark left in the morning before anyone was up.

I told Mom I couldn't do this anymore and cried in her arms. She talked to Dad and he reluctantly agreed to help us pack so we could leave with them as soon as possible. My heart soared. They cared. *They're really going to help us; I have a way out. Thank You, God.*

"Mommy, where are we going with all our stuff?" Michael asked as I packed his clothes in a suitcase.

"We're going to visit Grandma and Grandpa for the summer and have fun." I smiled.

"Yeah, let's go!" the boys yelled.

We packed our life in Mom and Dad's van and our car and we set out for Phillipsburg, Kansas. I hid my fear, sang songs, and talked to the boys so they believed we were going on a long summer vacation.

As we walked into my parents' home, the phone rang. I answered. "Mark, it's over. I won't live with a man who hurts his own boys," I blurted.

"What am I going to tell people?" Mark asked.

"I don't care what you tell them." I sighed. "Clearly, you're more worried about your reputation than us. I'm too mad to even talk to you." I slammed the phone down.

He called all day while I ignored his calls; I relented and talked to him that evening. "Darla, please don't hang up," Mark pleaded. "I'm sorry, I was just under stress. Can't you understand?"

"No." I hung up the phone. He called back for several days and I kept hanging up. "Lord, help me find some kind of answer or way to fix our marriage, please." Dad was clear—I was to stay married, even though he had seen how Mark treated me. His words shot through my heart, leaving me feeling helpless and hopeless. I knew I needed a different perspective so I called my parents' pastor. He counseled me to help find some answers. Should I get a divorce or was there any hope to save my marriage and my family? During our fourth session I gave the minister our whole history and waited for his response.

"Darla, from the description of your marriage, it seems to me Mark's an alcoholic. There's a rehab facility called Valley Hope in Norton. Maybe you should go there tomorrow and look around," Pastor Moore advised.

"I will. Maybe they can cure him, and he'll be okay." I thanked him and left.

The next day at Valley Hope, Tina, a woman counselor, talked with me extensively about Mark. She believed rehab might help him, if he embraced the program. She led me on a tour and I saw the effects of the patients' addictions in their shakes and sweats. I was terrified to learn these physical reactions were part of the detoxifying process the body goes through when the substance is taken away. Would Mark go through this process, I wondered? Several people's eyes revealed a sea of anger; others were dark and lifeless; still others acted as if nothing was wrong, reminding me of Mark. The reality of this place cemented the dangers, pain, and destruction of drugs and alcohol. I couldn't comprehend how Mark could make this choice. But maybe he didn't know. Surely by coming here and walking around, he'd see how bad he could get and choose to stop. "God, use me to help Mark heal and keep our family together," I prayed on my way to my parents' house.

I arrived at my parents' house full of hope and shared what I had learned. Mark could work to control his alcoholism. We were all relieved, especially Dad, since he reminded me again I was still Mark's wife in God's eyes. His words stung my soul.

Mark called several times, spouting blame and excuses. He finally let me talk and share what I had learned. In desperation, I declared the boys and I wouldn't come home again unless he went through treatment. Reluctantly he agreed to check into the rehab center but would need two days to make arrangements with his boss. He continued to deny he was an alcoholic because he didn't drink all the time. I didn't care what he called it as long as he went into treatment.

Finally, on a Friday, we drove into the Valley Hope parking lot; Mark was already waiting. The boys ran into his arms. My stomach churned.

"Daddy, we miss you," Joseph said.

"Are you going to get fixed?" Michael asked. The boys were old enough now at five and seven to express their sadness, anger, and confusion. Part of me was relieved while another part was afraid of

Mark's reaction.

"Yes, boys, I'll get better." He glared at me over their heads. We had a brief visit before he checked into Valley Hope, then the boys and I returned to my parents' house.

"Mommy." Michael looked at me in the rear view mirror. "Why can't we stay with Dad? Why does he have to stay in that place?"

"Your dad needs to stay there so they can help him fix his bad anger inside that comes out and hurts us." I looked back at the boys, safely strapped in their car seats.

"Mommy, can't we just be better so Dad will be better?" Michael reasoned.

"We're not the cause of your dad's anger and we can't fix him." I pulled off the road and parked. I turned to face them. "It's not our fault and nothing we ever do or say makes it okay for him to hurt us. It's wrong."

The pain and sadness of the boys pierced my heart deeper than I could have imagined. They wanted their dad and they, like me, were willing to take all the blame and the responsibility of his actions just so we could stay a family. They felt they were the cause of their dad's problems, just as I had accepted responsibility for making Mark mad and my mother ill. *Oh, God, please help me with my boys. Don't let them fall into the same guilt and shame of my life or follow the same path as Mark.*

I looked out the window, realizing with surprise we were still parked on the shoulder of the highway. "Boys, we have a choice to be mad and sad, or we can choose to be happy and make the best of our days with Grandma and Grandpa D. Which one will it be?"

"Happy," replied the boys in unison as we drove back to Phillipsburg. We sang along with the music on the radio; I thanked God that no matter what was going on in our lives, at some point I could eventually get the boys to laugh. My heart saw a glimmer of light and hope that Mark would finally find the root of his anger, hope we would matter enough for him to want to change, and hope we would finally be a happy family.

The counselor at Valley Hope asked me to attend fifteen hours of counseling per week split between individual, couples, and group sessions. My counseling focused on helping me learn about substance abuse and how to deal with life after rehab. I learned the motion and power of substance abuse cycles, and I saw my part in keeping the cycle going. By changing my actions and reactions I could stop being a victim or an enabler and choose to act in a healthy way. I decided I was done with those roles.

Two weeks went by without penetrating Mark's hardened, angry heart. Tina greeted me with a frown as I arrived in the morning. She told me Mark decided he didn't need the full thirty days of treatment so he was in the process of checking out. I asked her if he was ready to leave and she replied no, but only Mark could make that decision since his stay wasn't court ordered. She suggested I try to convince him to stay.

We briskly walked across the courtyard and entered her office. "Mark, what are you doing?" I questioned.

"I'm all better now, and I need to get back to work. I've stopped drinking, I understand I've messed up, I've apologized, so now we can go home. I've done what you wanted and it's time to go," he answered confidently.

"Tina, is he all better and ready for life?" I asked.

"No, Darla, he's not," she answered, turning to Mark. "Mark, you are near a breakthrough; if you leave now, statistics show you have a one in ten thousand chance of staying sober," she finished.

"Well, Mark, if you choose to leave now, the boys and I are not coming. You said you would go through rehab and that means all thirty days of it. I know this isn't easy and you're scared, but you have to find the root of your anger. Until that's fixed, you won't be 'all better.' You're not getting away with doing just enough to get by this time. We've played this game for ten years already and I'm done, so choose wisely," I challenged him.

He glared at me, turned around, slammed the pen on the release papers, and stomped out of Tina's office.

Several more days in treatment passed and he was still angry. I was losing hope. After a male group session Mark told me he had found some reasons for his anger, and he was sure he would be fine now. I asked him if he would like to share them with me so I could understand, but he refused. He said I'd see he had taken care of them. He patted my hand and gave me an unfamiliar warm smile; his attitude continued for his last week in treatment. I hoped I was witnessing a miracle and he was going to love us.

"Oh, thank you, God, for this breakthrough and for healing our future," I prayed silently on the return trip home to Wyoming after treatment. Mark was calm, talked with us, and spent time playing appropriately with the boys. Something had changed, but deep inside I wasn't sure I could trust him yet.

Chapter 20

"Life begins on the other side of despair."
—Jean-Paul Sartre

Within a few weeks Mark was transferred again to a jobsite in Nebraska. I welcomed this new start and the chance to be closer to our families. We packed our belongings and moved. I brimmed with new hopes to have a husband who cherished me, who was a great father and role model for his sons. I wanted a life and family full of love and laughter instead of pain.

The stress of the move and all of the changes revealed Mark's anger wasn't gone. Within a few days in Nebraska he reverted back to yelling, punching things, shoving me, and drinking. The boys were terrified and sad.

"Mom, what did we do to make Dad mad again?" The boys asked, fear in their eyes.

"You didn't do anything wrong." I hugged them. "I'll take care of you." I grabbed at reasons and excuses to ease their minds, but I couldn't put any of them into words anymore. I had to face the reality that Mark hadn't changed. It had just all been an act once again. I put the boys to bed and peeked in on them. "God, please help me. Show me what to do. I need your help, again," my heart screamed as I shut their door.

My mind searched for a way out of my marriage while my body went through the motions of taking care of Mark and the kids. However, I was also working ten hours a week for an insurance company. Because his utility company office shared the reception area and he could keep an eye on me, Mark allowed me work there.

Early one morning I received a call from the babysitter telling me she was sick. I picked up the phone to call work, but Mark grabbed the phone from my hand and hung it up. "The boys are old enough to watch out for themselves," he declared, pointing his finger at me. "You have to let them grow up or they'll turn out to be sissies."

"They are only seven and nine." I raised my hands in the air.

Mark grabbed my wrist. "You can ride to work with me willingly or I will drag you, but you're going." The boys witnessed our confrontation and begged me to go. They promised to be good for three hours. Everything within me said to stay, but I couldn't put the boys in the middle of our battle. I climbed into the pickup with Mark, worried, furious, and on guard.

Two hours later, the office phone rang and Mark answered it. He heard the boys fighting and slammed the receiver down.

"I'll go home and take care of the boys," I said, getting up from my desk.

"What are you going to drive, Stupid? You came with me." Mark shoved me back in my seat. "I'll take care of it."

Mark marched out the door. My heart raced and my mind spun out of control. What would he do to the boys? How could I let him leave? *Oh, God help me.* I ran to the bathroom and vomited. The receptionist, Nancy, came to check on me and helped me back to my chair. She was shocked at the way Mark reacted and treated me. My heart told me something terrible was happening, and I wasn't there to stop Mark. I was a horrible mother. I begged Nancy to give me a ride home and she agreed.

Our house was only five minutes away, but it seemed like an eternity. By the time we reached our house, panic saturated me. I ran from her car to the front door, yanked it open, and heard the soul-wrenching sobs of my sons. As I ran toward their bedroom, Mark came around the corner and clenched my arms in his hands, whirling me around to face him. "You won't give Joseph any babying this time, you bitch," he snarled.

"He's only seven," I cried, trying to break free.

He tightened his death grip on my arms and pulled me to his face. "He got what he deserved for breaking the rules, and if you talk to him or go to him before tomorrow, I will make sure you can't go to him again."

"What did you do? You monster, let me go!" I kicked him to escape.

"You bitch." He slapped me, threw me to the floor, dragged me into the bedroom, and slammed the door. "You stay in there or else." The memory of him holding a gun to my face and choking me time after time through the years flooded my mind, paralyzing me with fear. The look in his eyes assured me he would kill me this time if I left the room. That would leave my boys alone with him. I had to get the boys out. At that moment I remembered that I was to meet my parents tomorrow and send the boys home with them for their first summer visit. If I endured this torture and remained alive, I could deliver them to safety. Joseph's heart-shattering sobs ripped at my heart for hours. I wept and prayed for forgiveness for not coming home with Mark, for not stopping him, for not leaving Mark years ago. "God, I can't do this anymore."

I awoke on the floor and peered out the window to see Mark's pickup was gone. We were safe. I opened the bedroom door to find Joseph peeking out of his. He ran into my arms, his tentacles of anguish extending through my soul. I recognized the searing pain in his eyes. *How could I let this happen? What kind of a monster am I?* I rocked Joseph in my lap for a long time, hoping to soak up his despair. "Are you okay?" He nodded yes; pure devastation reflected the opposite in his eyes. "Joseph, can I do anything to help you?" Tears streamed down my face.

"No." He hugged me tight and cried.

Once we composed ourselves, I asked him if he still wanted to go and visit Grandpa and Grandma D. He replied yes, but he wanted to take a bath first. We walked to the bathroom and I started the bath water. I helped Joseph take off his shirt from yesterday and he turned his back to me. I gasped, engulfed his little body, and wept. The marks, those black, bulging, crimson marks from his head to his toes! *Oh, God! How could I let this happen to him? I have to kill Mark. God, I can't do this. Help me.* My anger, guilt, and shame overwhelmed me and poured out in tears for a long time.

"Mommy, I'm sorry I was bad. I'm sorry. I'll be good. You'll see," Joseph cried.

"Joseph, Mommy's so sorry Dad hurt you. You did nothing to deserve this, nothing. He was wrong to beat you," I whispered.

The sounds of our sorrow brought Michael to the bathroom doorway. Michael stared at us, devastated and tearful. I held out my arm and he ran to me and sobbed. "I'm sorry Dad hurt Joseph and you.

I was afraid to help you. There was nothing you could have done to help Joseph." Michael's eyes revealed utter disbelief and helplessness at the sight of Joseph's beating marks. We held on to one another for life until we were strong enough to go on.

I buckled the boys into the car and did my best to play happy music and visit with them to get their minds away from the trauma of last night. The boys became excited and happier the closer we got to Fort Collins, Colorado. Dad and Mom moved there six months prior and I was excited to have them closer now more than ever. When I met Mom and Dad they knew from the look on my face something terrible had happened, but they didn't ask and I didn't offer. I left my sons with Mom and Dad, relieved they were safe; I was ready to end their torture.

I returned home and found Mark waiting for me, watching TV, a beer in his hand. They were right at Valley Hope; Mark wasn't ready to quit drinking and I doubted he ever would be. I walked into the living room and sat at the opposite end of the couch, glaring into his eyes. "How could you pulverize your own seven-year-old son while your nine-year-old son watched?" I barked, trying to maintain my composure. "Nothing a child does could ever warrant a beating like that. Nothing!"

"He shouldn't have started the fight," Mark replied, emotionless. "He was wrong and I made damn sure he'll never do it again."

"You have a justification for everything bad you've ever done to the boys and me," I seethed, raising my voice and pointing my finger at him. "You've tortured, manipulated, and terrified people into submission and shrugged it off as your right to prove a point. Is that

142

what you call love? Do you love them? Have you ever loved them?" I hissed.

After a few moments of silent pondering, he peered indifferently into my eyes. "You know, I'm not sure. I guess I'll just have to learn to love them in the future."

My world came to a screeching halt at his words, "I guess I'll just have to learn to love them." Their sound echoed in my heart; every syllable sliced through my heart like a jagged icicle. *He doesn't love his own flesh and blood. What has he been doing for the last nine years of his sons' lives, besides using them to relieve his anger?* All this time I had held out with hope that somewhere deep down inside he loved us, but I was wrong, dead wrong. *I've kept us in hell for nothing.*

Mark stood up and walked over to me. He planted himself to tower over me and pointed his finger in my face. "The boys are mine. They belong to me, just like you."

I shoved him away, stood up, and shouted, "They're not cars you can beat up and discard, and neither am I. You disgust me."

He gripped his hands around my throat and lifted my ninety-five-pound body off the floor, shaking me like a rag doll. "Listen, bitch, you are one to talk. Miss High and Mighty, never-do-anything-wrong, pansy-maker. You're fat, ugly, and a worthless wife." Mark flung me through the air, body-slamming me to the floor, knocking the breath out of me, then stormed out of the house.

"That's it, God. He's going to die," I vowed. My boys are safe and now it's time to blow Mark's head off. My hands trembled as I dialed Mom's phone number.

"Hello," Mom said.

"Mom, tell the boys I love them, and I'll see them tomorrow," I said.

"Darla, what's wrong?" Mom asked.

"I'm taking care of everything. I love you all." I hung up the phone. I walked to the gun cabinet, pulled out a shotgun, loaded both barrels, and took my position in the chair facing the door. "God, if you don't make a way, I will," I stated. I flipped the safety off. My finger rested on the trigger.

Staring at the end of the barrels pointed at the door, I realized my happily-ever-after fantasy had turned into a nightmare. Mark wasn't my prince; he was my prison warden and I was his prisoner. I tried to fix him and me. I did my best to be understanding, forgiving, and submissive, because that's what God, my parents, and the church told me a good Christian wife should be. I've loved God all my life and yet I still ended up here. Tears rolled down my face. "God, I'm not worthy of saving, but my boys are. Help me." I clutched the cold steel of the double barrels. I had to kill Mark, our horror, once and for all.

The morning sun jolted me awake from my nightmare to see the shotgun in my hand; I quickly laid the gun down. At that moment I made the decision that I wouldn't turn into Mark by inflicting pain or death on someone else. *I have to take care of the bundles of love God entrusted to me.* The warm sun was beaming through the windows, warming my icy heart.

My thoughts cleared and I felt God speaking to my heart. "Darla, I've made a way. This is not your battle. Go home and be with your sons," I heard my spirit say. I grabbed my purse and rushed out the door. I felt a strong desire to speak with Pastor John, my pastor for the past three months. I drove to his office and rushed inside. He led me to a chair. "Darla, what's going on? You look like you're in trouble."

"Pastor John, two days ago Mark beat Joseph to a pulp when I wasn't there," I cried. "I took the boys to my parents and came back and confronted him yesterday. He hurt me and left the house. I told God He needed to make a way or I would. I waited all night with a shotgun to kill Mark and end the pain for all of us."

"Oh, Darla, I'm so sorry." He put his arm around me. "God protected you and made a way by not letting Mark come home last night. Go home to Colorado and let God deal with Mark." He took my hand and led me to the couch and reached for his Message Bible. He opened the pages to Ephesians 5:21–28 and read, "Out of respect for Christ, be courteously reverent to one another. Wives, understand and support your husbands in ways that show your support for Christ. The husband provides leadership to his wife the way Christ does to his church, not by domineering but by cherishing. So just as the church submits to Christ as he exercises such leadership, wives should likewise submit to their husbands. Husbands, go all out in your love for your wives, exactly as Christ did for the church—a love marked by giving, not getting. Christ's love makes the church whole. His words evoke her beauty. Everything he does and says is designed to bring the best out of her, dressing her in dazzling white silk, radiant with holiness. And that is how husbands ought to love their wives. They're really doing themselves a favor—since they're already 'one' in marriage."

Pastor John wasn't describing my husband's love; it was nowhere close.

He continued, "I love how the Message Bible brings God's word to everyday language. It helps us understand God's true view on marriage and submission. Many people and churches talk primarily about women's submission and leave out the responsibilities of the husband." I nodded my head in agreement. "God asked both of you to promise to love and cherish one another as you would the Lord. Darla, according to the scriptures, Mark should treat you with the utmost love and respect, making your submission easy. You can only hold up your end of the commitment."

"So, I'm not bound to Mark forever?" I asked.

He shook his head. "No, especially where abuse is concerned."

"If I divorce Mark, will God be mad at me?" I asked.

He placed his hand on mine and looked at me. "Darla, God says divorce is a sin. But God is clear about how we are to treat each other in the commitment of marriage and this can only be done in the grace of forgiveness given to all through the sacrifice of Jesus. He paid for our sins. I don't believe it's your responsibility to sacrifice yourself or your children to change or save Mark. There's only one Savior and that's Jesus. You gave Mark thirteen years to change. Now it's time to see an attorney. When you talk to him, use a hypothetical friend in your same situation so his advice is for the hypothetical friend. Then he won't call the police. The law would require him to report the abuse if you admitted your children were the abused. His counsel will help you decide your next step. Now, run, flee, and God will make a way." He hugged me good-bye.

I've lived in hell on earth because I believed in the half truths about marriage other people told me. "Oh, God, forgive me for putting my children through this and for my divorce. From now on I will read Your whole truth myself. God, You made a way, and I will take it."

I don't remember the attorney's name, but his words of advice for my hypothetical friend rang loud and clear. Since the mother had never filed child or spouse abuse charges against her husband to put him in jail, she would need to flee the state with them or Social Services would take her children from her.

I got in my car, buckled up, and began my three-hour journey to my parents' home in Colorado. I was leaving my entire life behind with no money and no extra clothes. I drove in silence for miles before I turned on the radio to hear a mixture of contemporary Christian music and hymns. Peace began to permeate my soul as the music soothed my mind and ministered to my broken heart.

Tears blurred my vision and I had to pull off the road as the words reverberated in my soul. "God, I don't doubt You, but I doubt there's any good in me. I've been a horrible mother. Please give me the courage to find You at the end of me. I need You to save me and set me free. I need You, Jesus."

I wiped my eyes and continued driving. My mind tossed with shards of guilt. I wondered if my boys would be better off if I ran into the ditch and went on to heaven. The road ahead began to blur and I shook my head. What was I thinking? That would be handing them to Mark. I rummaged on the floor for a rag, blew my dripping nose, and wiped my eyes. *I have to take care of the boys. They have no one else but me, and maybe Erma.*

Chapter 21

"You can avoid reality, but you cannot avoid the
consequences of avoiding reality."
—Ayn Rand

As I reached the edge of town I decided to go to Erma's house where I had always been welcomed with loving arms. I couldn't risk being rejected and have Mom and Dad tell me again I had to return to Mark. I pulled into her driveway and ran to the door. Erma opened it and caught me in her arms.

"Darla, I've been watching for you. I talked to Dolly and she said something was terribly wrong. You're so frail. When was the last time you ate?" Erma helped me to the kitchen table. She heated a teapot on the stove and pushed a plate of cookies toward me. Erma sat beside me, encasing me in love like she had done so many times in my past. Her house still glowed with love.

"I waited with a shotgun in my hand ready to kill Mark, Erma." I shook and sobbed. "I went to see our minister and he gave me scriptures that set me free," I panted. "The lawyer said Social Services would take the boys away from me if I stayed. The boys can't be hurt anymore."

"Darla, slow down and start from the top." Erma sat beside me and held my hand. I told her how Mark beat Joseph and, between anguished sobs, described the last few years of my hell on earth.

I heard the stories of my pain as I spilled the truth to Erma; I knew I did the right thing one minute and questioned my decision the next.

"Was I wrong to leave?" I looked at Erma through tears.

Erma placed her hands on my cheeks and gazed into my eyes. "I know how much you wanted this to work, but now you need to do what's best for the boys and you."

"How can I take care of them? I'm a worthless failure," I whimpered. "How will they be okay without a dad in their lives?" I cried.

"Don't confuse the ability to make a baby with the love, protection, and cherishing sacrifice of a true dad, like Paul," Erma said. Tears streamed down my face. I realized my boys felt my same pain because they weren't protected or cherished by their dad either. Erma hugged me close. She knew my pain and reminded me that I'd seen the way a good dad like Paul corrects his children without abusing them. "Do you want the boys to repeat Mark's behavior or do you want to show them a healthy way to live?"

"They can't repeat Mark's mistakes, they just can't." I grabbed my head to stop the thought. "I've allowed enough damage to be done to them. Oh, Erma, what kind of a mother am I to allow such pain?"

"You've been the best mother you could be at any given moment with the skills you possessed and the resources and support you had, which were none," Erma stated emphatically as she hugged me. "If it weren't for you, the boys wouldn't know love. You love them with all your heart. You've tried to protect them and fix yourself and Mark, and now you realize you can't do it. Would you be willing to talk to someone who helps abused women?"

I sat up, took a deep breath, and composed myself. "Yes. I need to know what to do next."

Erma went to the counter and wrote a phone number on a piece of paper and handed it to me. "This is the safe house where I trained last year. Call them and follow their directions; I can't go with you. This must be your decision. I'll be here when your mom brings the boys over."

I stared at the receiver, took a deep breath, and dialed the number. I introduced myself to a lady named Alice and told her my story. She assured me I called the right people and asked me to come to the safe house. To keep all the other women there secure, I was to follow her directions exactly. I agreed. She cautioned me to watch in my rearview mirror for anyone who might be following me, because my husband could have hired someone to find me. I wrote down the directions, hugged Erma, and ran to my car. Fear grew with every glance in the rearview mirror. Mark said he'd kill me if I ever divorced him. When I was with him, at least I knew where he was and what mood he was in. "God help me," I whispered and took a deep breath.

The directions ended at a two-story white Victorian house. I walked to the front door and rang the bell. A woman with bright blue eyes and a large smile opened the door. She placed her hand on my shoulder and introduced herself as Dena. I followed her through several hallways sprinkled with other women and children. They were talking and playing in an ordinary way, yet I realized the fragments of their lives were suspended, just like mine. We reached her office and she asked me to sit down in one of two overstuffed brown chairs. She sat in the other. "Tell me what brings you here."

I sat down and toyed with the fringe of a blanket draped over the arm. "I left my husband because he hurt my two sons. I don't know what to do to get away and how to protect the boys."

"Can you tell me how he hurt the boys?" she looked compassionate.

I glanced at her and stared at the floor. I was afraid of her condemnation and rejection when I revealed the secrets in my life, but I had no other option than to take a chance and share the truth. "Mark started when the boys were just infants and toddlers. He spanked them to extremes." I cleared my throat, searching for strength. "When my oldest son was five, Mark threw a baseball so hard it knocked the wind out of him. While I was gone, he kicked Joseph across the room into the bedpost and cut his eye. He was only three." I shifted in my seat and tears flooded my eyes.

Dena clasped my hand and leaned toward me. "Darla, I know this is painful, but I need to know what happened so I know how to help you. You are safe and you can do this."

"Five days ago he beat Joseph with a belt buckle until his backside was covered with welts and bruises from his neck to his toes," I gasped. "Mark wouldn't let me go with him. I couldn't stop him. How could I let this happen?" I sobbed uncontrollably for awhile.

Dena squeezed my hand. "Darla, you did the best you could with what you knew at the moment. The important thing is what you're doing now to protect the boys and yourself." She handed me a tissue and waited for my cries to subside. As I blew my nose Dena reached for a piece of paper. "Do you know the formal definition of abuse?"

I shook my head no. "I went through Valley Hope with Mark four years ago for his alcoholism, but no one talked to me about abuse."

Dena raised her eyebrows. "It should be a standard practice." She cleared her throat with a look of disapproval and sighed.

"Would it be okay if I read you the definition of abuse?"

I nodded in agreement.

She began.

- Does he call you or your children bad names?
- Does he lie and break promises continually?
- Has he punched walls, slammed doors, or broken belongings?
- Does he get in your face?
- Has he shoved, pushed, bruised, cut, scraped, or choked any of you?

"Mark has done all these things for years. I just thought he was in a bad mood and it was my job to make him happy." I took in a deep breath and felt the volcano of anger I kept boiling under the surface bubbling up.

Dena squeezed my hand. "The truth and knowledge of abuse brings the anger you're feeling. Let me continue and then we will talk, okay?" Dena waited for my nod.

- Does he give you the silent treatment or use guilt to get his way?
- Does he drink, use other drugs, or pick fights?
- Does he hurt your pets?
- Does he threaten to take the children away or abandon you?
- Has he isolated you from friends and family or prevented you from accessing any support system?
- Does he threaten to harm himself or others?

- Does he force you to have sex or touch you when you don't want him to?

- Has he threatened to kill you?

She looked at me, placing the paper in her lap. Every statement compounded the years of suffering into rage for Mark and condemnation for myself. "I can't believe how stupid I was." I smacked my head and threw my hands in the air. "What's wrong with me that I couldn't see this abuse? Why did I ever question leaving him?"

"Darla, be kind to yourself as you discover the truth." Dena patted my shoulder. "Would it be all right if we searched further to see what blinded you from the truth?" I nodded yes. "What was your lifelong dream?" Dena studied my eyes.

"To fall in love, get married, and have a family of my own to love." I stared into her eyes.

"And live happily ever after, right?" Dena added as tears rolled down my face. "Stay with me, Darla; there's a point to these questions. Once the truth is revealed, you'll be free. Did you have a favorite fairy tale?"

"I had two, Snow White and Cinderella. They were both able to take hard situations and still remain kind and joyful." I turned toward her. "Why?"

"What happens when real life doesn't match the fairytale life you dreamed in your head?" Dena asked, waving her hand in the air like a fairy godmother with a wand. I shrugged my shoulders.

"Have you seen Beauty and the Beast?" Dena asked.

"Yes. I don't like it." I shook my head. "He took her away from her family and isolated her. He was mean to her." I buried my face in my hands and cried for a few minutes. "In the end he became good, but my beast never did. I wanted my prince to love, cherish, and take care of me. I wanted my happily ever after. I tried to fix him and change him, but nothing worked. My life wasn't supposed to turn into a horror show." I shook my head and ran my fingers through my hair.

"Fantasy is a powerful thing when it collides with reality." Dena placed her hand on mine and I looked into her eyes. "You don't know what you don't know. Knowledge is power to understand and your own will, hope, and belief in God help you make and carry out a plan. Your mind kept you in fantasy to give you a way to cope with all your pain and still retain hope." I squeezed her hand. "The reason you feel torn is because you're still in love with the happily-ever-after fantasy, not with Mark. You have to let go of the fantasy to live in reality. Once you do, you can have a happy, healthy life. When you ask why questions, you just create shame and guilt that keep you down. Ask yourself what, how, and when questions to move forward." Dena patted my hand.

"Darla, you've told me about Mark's abuse to the boys. Can you tell me about Mark's abuse to you?"

"Mark hurt me a lot, mostly in secret. Maybe sometime we can talk about it, but right now I want to make sure the boys are safe and I have done everything I could have done." Guilt and shame shadowed my heart. "What are the chances Mark could be cured?" I asked.

"When a husband's been abusive for thirteen years and shows no desire to change, the chance in real life is none. Mark's an adult and can make his own decisions, but the boys can't. If you don't show the boys a healthy way to handle their anger, there's at least an eighty percent chance they will abuse their own children. They will do what they know. Can you live with your sons cloning Mark?"

Images of the boys as adults caught in the same anger and pain, using it to strike out at their children, left me breathless. I sat up and took a deep breath. "I can't change the past, but with God's help, I will change our futures. What do I need to do?"

Dena suggested the boys and I come for counseling once a week. She handed me a list of group sessions and a second paper with the names of several attorneys on it. "Call and make an appointment to get emergency custody and protection orders for the boys and you."

"I don't have any money," I replied. I was wearing the only clothes I had with me, and I'd fled with only the thought of escape. The few dollars of cash Mark allowed me were all that I had in my purse.

"The lawyers work pro bono. That means for free." She smiled. "Make sure you connect with him. He holds your lives in his hands. If you don't see him fighting for you, fire him and find another one." I took the papers, thanked her, and hugged her good-bye.

My revelation of truth connected my need for love, my religious misinterpretation, and my desire to live happily ever after. Its clarity severed the steel wires of fear and guilt twisted around my mind and soul that bound me to Mark. I was free. On my drive back to Erma's, I smiled and looked heavenward with fresh hope and a new grasp on life.

I ran into Erma's house and told her Dena smacked me into reality. "She helped me see my doubts stemmed from being in love with the happily ever after fantasy in my head, not with Mark," I blurted in my excitement.

Erma hugged me and looked into my eyes. "I'm glad you went. Mark called, and he's mad."

"No doubt, but I'm ready." I pushed my shoulders back and chest out. "It's over because he's still the beast and I refuse to be in the nightmare one more minute of my life." Erma smiled at my announcement.

The phone rang and I answered.

"Darla, what the hell are you doing?" Mark yelled.

"I'm filing for divorce as soon as possible," I announced.

"What am I going to tell everyone?" Mark asked.

These same words echoed from the past. "Tell them I'm on vacation. Tell them I was a spy and fled the country. I don't care what you tell them. From now on my concern is the safety and welfare of the boys. I'm over my fantasy with you, I'm over my love for you, and I'm over my life with you. You'll hear from my attorney." I slammed the phone down and felt a surge of confidence that had beckoned to me from the distance for years.

Within seconds the phone rang again and I answered, "Hello."

"Darla, I'm sorry," Mark started.

"I've heard thirteen years of excuses, torture, and brutality and all your chances are gone," I ranted. My mind was clear for the first time in many years and my anger found the right place to land.

"You bitch. I've given you everything you needed. You've never had to work and this is how you repay me by stealing my boys? They're mine, and I'll get them back. I told you in the beginning I would kill all of you before I let you have them in a divorce," he screamed.

"You'll have to kill me, because I'll protect them until I die," I screamed back. Erma grabbed the phone from my hand and hung it up.

Erma hugged me tight, pulling my arms to my sides. "Darla, stop. You're mad and hurt. Don't jump back into the abuse cycle." She led me to the table and sat beside me. "You need to give all your time and energy to focus on ways to keep you and the boys safe and start your new lives. Get your head on straight for the boys' sake and show them a healthy way. What's your next step?"

"I'm not sure I even know what healthy looks like after all these years." I glanced at Erma. "I've made such a mess of all our lives. I'm not sure I'm strong enough to raise my boys alone. How do I even begin?"

The front door opened, and the boys ran into my arms, Mom close behind them. "Mommy, when are we going home?" Michael said.

"Yeah, Mommy, when?" Joseph said.

"Boys, I need to talk to you." I held their hands, led them to the living room couch, and sat between them. I glanced at each of them and took a deep breath. "Boys, we're not going back home to live with your dad."

"Why?" Michael pushed me away and glared at me. "We love Dad and he loves us."

"Boys, your dad's angry and he hurts us and that's not love." I held Joseph's hand and reached for Michael's.

Michael swatted my hand away. "I want to go home."

"You boys deserve a safe and happy place to live. It won't happen with your dad. I'm sorry for all the bad and hurtful things you've felt. I won't let you live another minute in pain and fear." The tears in their eyes drew the tears from mine. Joseph pressed close to me and Michael soon huddled in and sobbed. They couldn't hide from the pain no matter how much they loved their dad.

Through my heartache and tears I saw Mom and Erma holding one another at the end of the couch. They heard everything and stayed to support us.

"Maybe if we're better, Dad won't hurt us." Michael looked up at me. Michael was trying to fix things, copying my example.

I knelt on the floor so I could look up into both the boys' eyes. "Boys, none of this is your fault. You are good boys and you never did anything to deserve the hurt and pain your dad gave you. It's not your fault. He's the one who's sick and it's his fault. Do you understand?"

"No. Dad said it was all my fault. I'm sorry, Mommy." Joseph fell sobbing into my arms with Michael following. Mark had convinced all three of us that it was our fault he was mean. Watching my boys' anguish brought back all the memories of pain from my own childhood. We all clung to one another and sobbed.

Oh, God, I can't bear their pain. Please help me know what to say and how to help heal their broken hearts. I have to be strong. I composed myself. "Joseph, everyone does bad things, but they never deserve to be beaten, kicked, or punched by anyone. Parents should correct their children, not hurt them or call them names." I wiped the tears from their eyes and hugged them close. "Even if you never did a thing wrong, your dad would hurt you because of his bad anger inside." I lifted their chins until our eyes met. "You didn't cause your dad's bad anger. Do you boys understand?" They huddled in tight.

Michael cried for a few minutes before he pushed me away, stood up, and yelled, "I want to go home! You told us we'd go home! You're a liar! I hate you!" He lunged at me, his fists flailing.

I scooped Joseph up and placed him on the couch, then spun around to collide with Michael's anger. I reached both arms around Michael to keep him from punching me. "Michael, I know you're mad and sad, but I won't allow you to use your fists to vent your feelings. I love you and I'll hold you until you're safe." Within seconds Michael collapsed in sorrow as I held him to my heart. "Boys, I'm sorry your hearts are breaking." I gathered Joseph in my other arm. "I love you two, and it's my job to make sure you're not hurt anymore. And I can't let you hurt each other. That means we can't live with your dad. I'm sorry," I whispered while I cradled our heap of broken hearts and wept.

I knew the boys' angry words were their attempts to stop their anguish. It was hard for me to comprehend and deal with this turmoil as an adult; I couldn't imagine how much more incomprehensible it was for them. *God, help them.* Mom and Erma joined us in a group hug until we had no more tears.

We collected our broken hearts enough to watch some television and eat with Paul, Erma, and their girls. Mom wanted us to live with them, and I longed for this, too, but Dad needed a week to clean out two bedrooms for the boys and me. Paul and Erma insisted that we stay with them until my parents were ready for us. The boys and I settled in and I focused on the next steps I had to take to be free of Mark.

Chapter 22

"In what way can a revelation be made but by miracles?
In none which we are able to conceive."
—William S. Paley

The next day I pulled out the paper with the attorneys' names and made an appointment with Lance Olman. On my way to his office, my heart raced with every glance in the rearview mirror. The receptionist announced my arrival to Mr. Olman through the intercom. *What will he be like? I've never had to deal with a lawyer. Am I smart enough to understand the legal side?*

A few minutes later a giant man in a black pinstriped suit introduced himself and shook my hand. He led me down a hallway into his office and closed the door behind me. I took a seat as he walked behind his large cherry desk and took his. He glanced at me, his hand poised above his yellow legal pad. "To understand your case, I'll need you to tell me some incidents of the alleged abuse you endured."

At his words, I felt my face flush and the blood pound in my chest. I sat up, leaned forward, and stared at him until he looked at me. Once I had his full attention, I stood up and placed one hand on his desk, pointed my finger at his face. "Alleged abuse? Let's start with the time he violently shook a three-month-old baby, or when he threw a baseball so hard it knocked the wind out of his five-year-old son to prove he should pay attention, or when he kicked his three-year-old son across the room into a bedpost and cut his eye because he couldn't find his jacket."

Lance's eyes grew huge and he leaned back to create a safe space between us. I leaned in farther and waved my finger. "Oh, and when he refused to take his oldest son to the doctor for three days after he'd fallen and broken his arm because he needed to learn to be a tough man, or when he beat his youngest son with a belt buckle until his entire back side had welts from his head to his toes." Lance relaxed his shoulders, leaned forward, and held his hands up in surrender. "He calls his sons stupid, sissies, mama's boys, retards, and pigs to keep them from eating too much; he's punched, slapped, and choked me. He forced me to have sex, called me a worthless whore, slut, and bitch in front of the boys, and he held a shotgun to my head three weeks after we were married. You may call this alleged abuse. I call it my hell on earth. I've taken crap from Mark for thirteen years and I won't take anymore from anyone. Are you on my side or not?" I seethed through gritted teeth, glared at him with my hands on my hips, and waited for his response.

"Uh, clearly I asked the question wrong and I'm sorry." He held his hands open to me. "You've made a solid case of abuse, and I want to represent you if you'll give me another chance. Would you please sit down so we can talk?" He motioned for me to take a seat, but I crossed my arms, inhaled deeply, and studied him. He looked sorry and sincere and waited quietly for my response.

"I will keep you as long as you fight for me and my boys," I announced and then sat back down, still keeping my guard up.

"Fair enough." He nodded. "We'll file for emergency temporary custody orders tomorrow afternoon. I need you to write down all the

161

instances of abuse you just stated, and any other ones you can remember. Include the dates, where you were, and what was said." He saw my puzzled look. "The more details you can give me, the quicker you will get the orders." He wrote on his notepad and glanced up at me. "Does your husband have access to any firearms?"

"Yes. He's an avid hunter and has over a dozen guns." Lance froze and looked at me for a moment before he wrote more on his pad. I felt the tinge of fear hit my heart. "He constantly told me if I divorced him, he would find me and kill me and take the boys. How can we stop him?"

"I know you are scared and there are no guarantees in life, but a restraining order is the place to start." Lance got up and walked around the desk to sit in the chair next to mine. "Darla, I need to ask you if you ever had Mark arrested or reported any abuse to the authorities."

"No, I was too afraid." Tears welled up in my eyes and Lance touched my hand. "Why? Did I do something wrong?"

"Let's take this one step at a time. First, we need to file a request for emergency temporary custody orders to give you the authority to make all the decisions for the boys' welfare, school, doctors, or any other need. Then we'll file a restraining order so Mark can't come near you without being arrested." Lance smiled as I sat up straight. "You will need to become a resident of Colorado. That requires living here for ninety days. Because of your situation, you'll have to make sure no one finds you to serve you with court papers from Nebraska."

"Lance, what will happen to the boys if I get served papers?" Fear jolted my heart as I waited for his answer.

"Because you never filed formal charges against Mark, the Social

Services system would take the boys from both of you until they determined which parent was fit to raise them." He squeezed my hand and stood up. "But that's not going to happen, because you are a very smart and strong woman. Now go and write down the ammunition I need to fight for you. Be careful and watch out for anyone following you."

I stood up, thankful for his words of confidence. "Thank you, Lance. I'll be back tomorrow. I peered out the door, ran to my car, and glanced in the rearview mirror all the way home. This felt like a fugitive movie, except it was real life. "God, help me."

*   *   *

Over the last eighteen years, Erma and Paul had been raising their six adopted children. Their three middle girls were still living at home, and all three were sitting at the kitchen table when I returned from Lance's office. I told them I had to write down all the abuse evidence for my attorney, and he needed it by tomorrow. They volunteered to watch the boys and put them to bed so I would have the time and space I needed. I retreated to a bedroom in the basement and started to record the last thirteen years of my pain on a yellow legal pad Erma supplied.

I pressed my pen on the page and the dam where'd I'd held all the abuse inside for thirteen years ruptured, spewing enough incidents to fill the front and back of twelve pages of legal paper. I paused only for the sudden outbursts of anger, despair, and tears that were absorbed by a box of tissues. How could I have been so dumb and blind? I kept the fantasy that Mark would see our love and somehow magically love us, but he never did. I melted into a heap of molten shame. "God, how can

You forgive me? How will the boys ever forgive me? How can I forgive myself?" I wept from the depths of my soul through the night. I awoke early and took a shower to wash away last night's anguish and regain my self control. I helped the boys get ready for their first day of school and kissed them good-bye as I buckled them into Erma's car.

I was off to Lance's office to deliver the horrific record of my married life to Lance. He escorted me to his office and I took a seat while he closed the door. I handed him my tattered life. He skimmed through the incidents with an occasional raised eyebrow and glance at me. He finished the first page and put the papers on the desk. He stood up and walked around to take a seat next to me. Lance encased my quivering hand with his. "I'm sorry you had to relive this. I'll have the orders ready after lunch. The details you provided tell the horrible truth. I know the judge will grant emergency temporary custody and a restraining order. Is there anything else I can do for you?"

"If Mark doesn't catch me, will I keep my boys?" I stared at him, empty inside.

"Yes. You're showing your primary goal is to protect your children. I've tried to help many women who want to leave their abuser, but their fear and need to have a man overrides their responsibility to take care of their children. I'm proud to defend the courageous woman you are."

I left the office numb and dazed. I drove straight home to find a gigantic vase with two dozen roses. My name was on the tag; I opened it. "Darla, I'm sorry for everything. I'll do whatever you want. Please call me. Love, Mark." I picked up the flowers, went out the back door, opened the trash bin, and dumped them in. I came back in the door to hear the phone ringing.

"Hello, Darla, did you get the flowers I sent I'm sorry I'll do whatever you want I want you back I love you and the boys of course," Mark blurted without a breath.

"I've filed for a restraining order on you and emergency temporary custody of the boys. It's over for us, and you'll only be able to see the boys under supervised visitation," I said.

"I'll take you down, you lying, manipulative whore. I have more money, and I'll take the boys from you. They'll know what a liar you are, and they'll hate you." He slammed the receiver down.

He has never changed and never will. My determination became steel. He would not win, not this time.

Chapter 23

"Once you bring life into the world, you must protect it.
We must protect it by changing the world."
—Elie Wiesel

I thought I should look respectable for court, so I dressed in black slacks and a nice shirt. I walked into the courtroom and sat next to my attorney. Mark's absence put me at ease. Lance approached Judge Chapman and handed him the request for emergency temporary custody, which would only let Mark see the boys under supervision, and a restraining order. He began a summary of the request but was interrupted by the judge's hand in the air.

Judge Chapman read in silence for a few minutes. He put the request down and stared at me. "The detailed descriptions of the alleged abuse incidents in a case like this are usually displayed by the condition of the plaintiff."

I bit my tongue to keep from screaming. How dare he sit up on his pedestal and tell me the last thirteen years of torture were a figment of my imagination? Maybe if I had a black eye, teeth knocked out, or I couldn't hold my head up, he would believe me.

"Your honor, the evidence is clear. My client's not on trial. She asks the court for protection for her children and herself, which the court has the obligation to provide given the threats on my client's life and the arsenal of weapons her husband has in his possession," Lance stated.

The judge shifted the papers and peered into my eyes. "I'll grant both requests, including the supervised visitation for the father, but I'll keep an eye on this case. You can pick up the papers in one hour. Next case." He pounded his gavel on the desk, dismissing me.

We exited the court room. "I can't believe he called me a liar. Do I have to die before he believes me? And if I'd shot Mark's head off, would he have believed me then?" I fumed.

"Darla, you're a strong, confident woman who fights back. The court doesn't often see women like you. You should take it as a compliment and use it to your advantage." He raised one eyebrow and smiled. "You have a ton of leverage on your side. Go home and I'll call you in a few hours with the orders." He veered to the left at the court house steps and I took a right.

Today was the start of my new life. I was ready for the fight. "God, give me Your strength and wisdom."

*   *   *

The first week as I stayed with Erma, Mom came over and spent many hours with me, sewing and sharing her heart. Mom understood the abuse; she'd lived it as a child. These precious times together chiseled away at the years of granite stone walls I'd erected between us as a result of the past pain. Mom had a fresh softness toward me I had never known.

Mom came over to Erma's to sew with me one afternoon. When we stopped for a break, Mom reached over and took my hand in hers. "I realize I didn't do everything right, Baby." She squeezed my hand. "I wish I could do things all over again starting from your birth. When you were born, I wasn't prepared to see a clone of myself. All I could see was the pain in my past when I looked at you." Tears streamed down her face. "At times I wanted to consume you with love or try to find your prince, but most of the time I hid from the pain of my past and from you. I'm sorry for all the heartache I caused you. You didn't deserve the way you were treated by me or your dad. I tried my best, but I realize it wasn't good enough. All I can say is I'm sorry. Can you ever forgive me?" She looked at me and cried.

Tears ran down my face. My mom loves me. She tried her best and she's sorry. My heart leapt with joy and freedom from the lies that she didn't love me. "Mom, I know you did the best you could, and I'm doing the best I can with my boys." I held her hands in mine and cried. "I forgive you. Please forgive me for any hurts I caused you."

"Baby, there's nothing to forgive you for." She wiped away my tears. "I could see a supernatural grace, mercy, strength, and joy God had given you in your heart amidst the pain in your life. He has blessed me with your love more than you know. I'm ashamed I wasn't able to give you my unconditional love that you needed and deserved. I'm sorry." She cried in my arms. "I want you to know you are the best mother I have ever seen and the one I wished I could have been. You would die for your boys, and you never backed down from protecting them. You love them the same and have no favorites. I should have told you this sooner. I'm sorry." We sobbed in each other's arms until our tears were gone.

"I love you, Mom. Everything's okay between our hearts." Inside my heart I thanked God for healing our relationship in pure love, for this miracle. "Mom, let's not spend time wishing our lives would have happened differently or we would have talked sooner. Let's enjoy our time together from now on." I smiled and hugged her.

Mom wanted to help, and I longed for the opportunity to make up for lost time. She said Dad had finally finished cleaning our bedrooms and she was angry with him for taking two weeks. I told her it didn't matter now, because we were coming home. The next day the boys and I moved in with Mom and Dad.

Mom and I talked, loved, and healed, but she still fell into her escape of illnesses. Every day Dad's subtle comments of anger toward me increased. One afternoon, after I laid the boys down for a nap, I joined Dad to watch a baseball game in the living room. Mom was in her room, sick in bed, again. Dad muted the game and turned to me. "Darla, can't you find some way to fix your marriage?"

I stared, paralyzed by the thought. I sat up and leaned forward. "Dad, I can fix me and my part, but I can't fix Mark. Lord knows I've tried." I inhaled and sighed. "I've told you most of what Mark did to me and the boys. How can you ask me to do this?"

Dad leaned back and glanced between me and the baseball game. I waited for our eyes to meet. My own father was willing to turn a blind eye to the abuse to his grandchildren and now to me. The sting of his rejection and abandonment reddened my face and crushed my heart.

I stood up and walked several steps away. I took a deep breath, turned to face him, and held out my hands. "I will never understand how you refused to protect me, your own flesh and blood, after I was raped or when Mark put a shotgun to my head. Do you remember telling me I'd made my bed and I had to lie in it?" Dad looked at me, tears pooling in his eyes. "Well, Dad, I almost killed Mark and left your grandchildren to fend for themselves. In my mind, dads are supposed to love and protect their daughters. Instead, you can't seem to get rid of me fast enough." I wiped my streaming tears and cleared my throat. "I've forgiven you, but I don't understand you. I can't make you love me, but I can stop you from hurting me and the boys again. Your innocent grandchildren and I will never go back to Mark to be hurt or killed."

Dad bit his lip and rocked in his chair. He swiped his eyes impatiently and looked at me. "I struggle with your vow to God because He hates divorce."

"God hates the act, not the person." I stared at him and sat back down. "I've talked to God and several ministers about the commitment Mark and I made to each other under Him. I kept mine and Mark didn't. He didn't treat me like Christ or love and protect me. He brutalized us."

I placed my hand on his and he looked at me. "Dad, I'm getting a divorce. The boys and I need to be around people who support us. I think it would be best if we go back to live with Erma and Paul." I stood up and walked toward my bedroom. I paused and turned around. "Dad, please do your best to show your grandsons you love them with kindness and good words. They need it more than ever."

I went to my room and packed. When the boys awoke, I was finished. I told them Grandpa and Grandma were too sick to have us stay with them so we were going to live with Paul and Erma. They helped me pack their things with sad hearts. Once we were packed, I eased into Mom's bedroom to tell her we were leaving. The former glaze of escape settled on her face when she heard the news. I kissed her and left with the boys through a familiar fog of disappointment. Dad didn't try to stop us from leaving. In the depths of my heart, I wished he would have shown he loved me in some way, just once.

Chapter 24

"Courage is not simply one of the virtues, but the form
of every virtue at the testing point."
—C. S. Lewis

A week after we moved in with Paul and Erma, Lance called me. He informed me he had just received a petition from Mark's attorney to arrange for unsupervised visitation in Nebraska. Because of the abuse, Lance requested that the supervised visitation currently in place in Colorado and weekly phone calls with the boys remain, along with private weekly counseling sessions for the boys to help them heal. With all the evidence, the court agreed. Mark was furious. During their phone calls, Mark would tell the boys not to talk to the counselor because he would mess with their minds and keep them away from him. The boys felt stuck, and I felt powerless because the phone calls were court ordered.

It had been thirty days since I left Mark and moved in with Paul and Erma. I relied on them to buy our food, clothes, and provide our shelter since Mark closed all the bank accounts. I felt guilty and decided I had to find a job to support the boys while remaining on the lookout for Mark. I found a job at Colorado State University in the kitchen of the dormitory where Erma worked. My supervisor and coworkers knew my circumstances and helped watch for anyone strange or new. Three weeks into the job, Erma ran into the kitchen, seized my arm, and pulled me toward the back door.

"Darla, two thugs are at the front desk asking for you." She peeked around the corner. "Sue's driving my car to the back door. I'll take you to a safe house because several other men are waiting at our house."

Sue pulled up to the back door and waited in the idling car. Erma peeked outside to make sure the coast was clear. I ran to the car's back door and dove under a blanket. Erma closed the door behind me and jumped in the front passenger seat. "Stay on the floor. We're going out the back way," Erma commanded, and Sue took off. "We'll pick up the boys and take you all to a safe house after we take Sue home."

I melted into the floor board. My heart jumped inside my chest. I felt like a fugitive in a getaway car en route to pick up my boys and disappear. My mind raced on our way to drop Sue off at her house. *I can't believe it's so hard to save my boys and myself from Mark and start a new life. What will I tell them? God, help me.*

The car stopped at the boys' school. Erma went inside to get them and they hopped in the back seat. "Mommy, why are you under the blanket?" Michael giggled. "Why are we out of school early?"

"I was trying to surprise you, but you're too smart." I peeked out. "We're going on a special trip and we'll be gone for a while," I answered.

"Is Dad coming?" Joseph asked.

"No, just the three of us." I sat up in the seat and hugged them.

Erma and I did our best to keep the boys' minds occupied for our two-hour ride to Wyoming. All our chatter failed to dispel the fear in the boys' eyes. Per Dena's instruction, Erma parked at the east side of the Wal-Mart parking lot, next to a blue Ford station wagon with a smiley face sticker on the bumper. A lady with brown hair emerged from the vehicle, walked up to us, and said her name was Sally and she was with the safe house. I breathed a sigh of relief. I got out and shook her hand and the boys followed. She asked us to say our good-byes. Sally's words paralyzed the boys with terror. The image of saying good-bye to Zafarrah flashed through my mind. I struggled to hold back the dam of pain and emotions waiting to burst forth. Erma embraced them and kissed them good-bye. I walked to the trunk and retrieved the suitcase we'd packed and stored in her car earlier for such an occasion. I hugged Erma and thanked her for saving us and for always being there for me. I inhaled my sorrow and choked back tears to keep my voice strong for the boys.

"I love you, Darla. I always have and always will. I'll be back to get you when it's safe." Erma wiped the tears from her eyes. "Take this time to seek God and love on the boys. Try to make it fun." She distributed one more round of hugs and drove off. We loaded the suitcase into Sally's trunk and got into the back seat together.

"Mommy, where are we?" Joseph asked.

"Why are we hiding?" Michael looked at me. "What did we do wrong?"

"We didn't do anything wrong. We're on our way to stay in a house for a while until it's safe for us to go back to Fort Collins. It's like the one you visit for counseling."

"Is Dad after us?" Michael asked.

"Your dad sent other people to find us, but we escaped." I smiled. "It will be okay, boys. I promise."

We stopped in an alley beside a tall white privacy fence locked with a keypad alarm. Sally pushed the buttons and the gate swung open to the back door of another white two-story Victorian house. We entered the locked back door to the mud room. I put our suitcase down and we shed our shoes and coats and put on worn slippers.

"Where are all the people like in the safe house in Fort Collins?" Michael asked.

"Right now there's no one here but you three. If anyone else needs our help, you'll have to share the house." Sally smiled. "For now it's yours and you're free to use anything in it. Let's see if we have ice cream." She reached in the freezer and pulled out two ice cream drumsticks and handed them to the boys, who sat dazed at the table.

"Boys, I know this is hard and I'll answer all your questions in a minute." I unwrapped their ice cream. "First I need to talk with Sally because she has to go." I followed Sally into the living room.

Sally told me I should find everything we need in the cupboards, but if we missed a vital supply, she gave me a phone number to call. I would find a bedroom upstairs with three beds so we could stay together to ease the boys' fears. "Sally, I never thought it would come to this." I ran my fingers through my hair.

"None of the women who stay here ever do." She hugged me. "Darla, keep fighting for yourself and your boys."

"I will. Thank you." I hugged her one last time before she left.

I locked the door behind her and turned toward the boys. "Mommy, I'm scared." Joseph walked to me and clutched my arm.

"Me too." Michael joined us. I walked with them into the living room and sat on the couch, a son nestled under each arm.

"Sometimes we get scared in life when things happen and the first thing we must do is pray. We held hands and closed our eyes. "Jesus,

175

help us be courageous in You and know what to do. Amen."

"What's courageous?" Joseph whispered.

"It's our ability to walk through our fearful thoughts, emotions, and uncertainty." I hugged them.

"Does courage make fear go away?" Michael said.

"No, with God's help courage gives you the strength to go through the scary things. Even in the middle of a frightening experience like this one, you choose to make the best of this situation or lie around and feel sorry for yourself." The boys slumped into the couch. I knelt on the ground to see their faces and waited for them to look at me. "Don't let fear, situations, or circumstances get you down in life. No one controls your spirit and attitude but you. You have my strong Native American warrior blood in you and God in your hearts, so be courageous." I smiled at them and they grinned back. "Now, who can beat me upstairs to explore this humongous house?"

"Me, Mommy," Joseph said.

"No, me." Michael took off for the stairs.

We explored the house and claimed our beds. We settled in the living room and made a castle from the couch cushions, draping some throw blankets over the ends. Snuggled safe inside our haven from the world, we watched "The Land Before Time."

The boys and I cried, played, laughed, and prayed for a week until it was time to move to the next safe house. I packed our lives in our small suitcase and loaded it and the boys into Sally's car. We drove to meet Erma at the Wal-Mart parking lot so she could take us to the next safe house. It was so good to see a loving face and know we were headed back home to Colorado.

Our next hiding place was back in Fort Collins with Paul and Cindy, long-time friends of Erma and Paul. Cindy would take the boys to and from school and I would stay alone with my thoughts, memories, regrets, guilt, and shame. It took all my faith and strength to keep positive and strong for the boys. I found help each week in my counseling sessions with Dena. I told her I would do everyday things and my thoughts would be instantly transported back to a horrible incident from the past, rendering me breathless. It was hard to control my emotions once the torment flashed in my head.

"I'm so mad at myself for not leaving sooner." I ran my fingers through my hair.

"What else do you feel?" Dena touched my arm reassuringly.

"Frustrated." I glanced at her, tears gathering. "Guilty, ashamed, defeated, and worthless."

"Can you remember the first time you felt these feelings?" Dena looked at me.

I took a deep breath, stood up, and exhaled. I glanced at her and began to pace the floor. I told her the story of when Mom first introduced me to the missionaries in Iran, unloading all my guilt and shame.

"Darla, I'm sorry you have felt so much pain." She held my hand until I composed myself. "Did you ever talk to your mom about your introduction?" Dena asked.

"Yes. When I was twenty-five I found the strength to talk to her about it." I wiped my face. "She was unaware and deeply sorry that her words hurt me so much, and she asked for my forgiveness. She never said those words again, but I still struggle with the guilt and shame, and strive to prove my value." I stood up again and began to pace the floor.

"The other deep blow happened when I was fifteen. I was raped and almost choked to death." I took a deep breath and continued. "That was horrible enough, but what Dad said to me after the attack demolished me." I cried for a few minutes before I shared his devastating words that I was used goods and he didn't know who would ever want me. I collapsed in her arms.

"Darla, I'm sorry, I can't imagine your suffering." She hugged me until I calmed down.

"These experiences and feeling abandoned so many times by my parents left me believing I was insignificant, condemned, and unworthy of my very existence. I was lucky to ever have any love or good in my life." I held my hands out to Dena and pulled them to my heart. "I tried for years to fix myself, Mom, Mark. In the process I hurt my boys. I can't fix anything. I feel unworthy to receive love. I'm ashamed of what I've done and what I've allowed my boys to go through and what I've become." I sobbed.

Dena placed her hand on my shoulder. "I would venture to say your mom is locked in the same cycle of guilt and shame, except she deals with it through her illnesses and mental seclusion. You've had guilt and shame modeled from your birth and that's the pattern you've followed," Dena said.

"How can I change my life?" I searched her eyes.

"You have, my dear," she smiled and patted my hand. "Your relationship with God has guarded the spark of hope and faith that somehow your life would be good someday. Given your background, it's a miracle you didn't snap and kill Mark. Instead, you placed your children's future first. You've been through many fires and you have come out strong and refined. You don't see it, but I do." Dena smiled. "It's normal to have flashbacks and feel emotions you've stuffed. You're changing your life and growing healthy. The old is battling the new. This takes choices, time, and practice, like building a muscle." Dena flexed her bicep. "Your normal has been a self-destructive cycle that landed you in my office. I would like to read a scripture to you from Romans 12:2." Dena waited for my nod. "'Do not conform to the pattern of this world, but be transformed by the renewing of your mind. Then you will be able to test and approve what God's will is— his good, pleasing and perfect will.' You need to set your mind to embrace the strangeness of a new, healthy way until it becomes your new normal. It just takes practice."

"Can't I control my flashbacks?" I placed my hands on my head.

"When they start, take a deep breath and say, 'I'm in the present. God, help use my past to bring me a joyful life.' You'll need to say this many times at the start. Once your subconscious realizes you're in charge, those flashbacks will lose their tormenting power. It may take years for these to go away and some may never totally leave. You're in charge, not your emotions or fears. It's your choice."

I hugged Dena and slipped out the back door. "God help me embrace Your life of love, grace, and mercy. Help me be the best me I can be for You and the boys."

The day of residency arrived. I ran out into the front lawn and rolled in the grass and lay in the sun, breathing in freedom. I was now a resident of Colorado and I was free to walk, run, and have a life without fear of Mark's detectives finding me, or constantly looking over my shoulder.

My emancipation brought back the feelings of my first weeks in America. It lasted for several days until Mark called to talk to the boys. The words I could hear Mark say and the boys' cold reactions toward me created a flood of overwhelming anger inside.

Erma motioned for me to sit next to her at the kitchen table, away from the boys. "Darla, don't you think Mark feels justified in his hate and anger, too?" I nodded. "Anger is a sign of pain and often unforgiveness. I understand your hurts, and so does God. The question I have for you is, 'What will you choose to do with your pain and anger?' God says our battle is in the spiritual realm. People are the vehicle Satan uses to deliver his evil. Once people open themselves up to his dominion through his twisted truths and power, they are at his beck and call. Mark's actions reveal who's in control of his life." She moved closer and put her arm around me. "Satan's a parasite with the main goal of multiplying more negative thoughts, emotions, and actions. If you don't kill them, they will grow, control, and destroy your life. You could end up mirroring Mark."

I stared at her in horror. She cupped my face with her hands and looked into my frightened eyes. "Darla, don't take the path of death. Choose life with God's love, forgiveness, and strength. Don't let Satan win by welcoming darkness into your heart through unforgiveness. You must forgive Mark, because Jesus died for your sins and forgave you."

"I can't pretend nothing happened." I raised my voice.

"Forgiveness is putting down the hurts of the past at the cross of

Jesus and leaving them there. It doesn't mean you have to forget. It's important to learn to keep healthy boundaries to have a relationship with an unhealthy person. Forgiveness means you take back the power you surrendered to the other person." Erma's words trickled into my soul. *God, I forgive Mark.* I started to feel the shackles fall away as God freed my soul.

I washed my face before bed and caught my angry reflection in the mirror. I still felt anger and unforgiveness as memories of the past abuse flooded my mind. "God, help me forgive Mark for all the hurt and pain he caused in my life and to the boys. Please release me from giving Mark any power over me. Lord, help me forgive myself for letting this happen. Help my wounds heal so I can have a loving heart," I sobbed. After a long time, I managed to take several deep breaths, exhaling the rage from my soul. I felt God's peace. The bondage of anger and resentment disappeared. Within minutes I felt no sadness, anger, or care where Mark was concerned. "Thank you, God, I'm free."

Chapter 25

"Change is the law of life. And those who look only to
the past or present are certain to miss the future."
—John F. Kennedy

For the first six months I bounced among work, counseling, being a mother, and court. Mark constantly fought to have the supervised visitation and counseling changed or stopped. I rented a house near Erma and Paul for support, but exhaustion, depression, and loneliness were my constant companions.

During the months of supervised visitation, Lance petitioned the court three times to extend the supervised visitation without success. At the end of the court-ordered time, it was clear I could no longer keep the boys' time with Mark in a controlled environment. Fear pierced my heart; I had to talk with Erma so I walked to her house. I opened the door and ran into her arms.

"Darla, what's going on?" Erma led me to the table.

"I just heard from Lance that the last attempt to extend supervised visitation was denied. The boys will have to visit Mark in Nebraska. The first visit is in a week!" Panic struck my heart. "I can't shake the feeling that Mark will hurt them again. Maybe if I run away with them, I could still protect them." I sat in silence for a few moments. "But, I'd be running forever and the boys would never learn to stand and fight," I remarked. Memories of what it was like to grow up without the love and support from family bubbled to the surface. "I can't control things anymore, can I?"

"No, Darla, it's time to let God have control. You have to trust that He will protect and help the boys." Erma held me while I cried.

"It breaks my heart to see the boys excited to be with Mark." I wiped tears from my cheeks. "I don't understand how they could want to be with him after all the abuse they endured from him. I just don't understand."

"Every young boy and girl wants to have their dad's love and approval no matter what has happened. You desired the same thing from your parents, even though they weren't there for you. Remember how long it took you to see Mark wasn't going to change? You can't fault them for hoping their dad has changed, can you?" Erma hugged me. "Darla, we must all travel through challenges we don't understand or can't control. However, the fires we encounter on the outside are not in control of the inside unless we let them. You alone have the choice and power to control the condition of your heart. We are called to do our best and release the rest to God through our faith and trust. He will give you the courage to go through this fire and keep the peace in your heart."

"He has so far." I hugged Erma and left.

A year after we separated, the time arrived when I had to meet Mark and exchange the boys for their first unsupervised visitation. The boys were now eight and ten years old. I helped them pack their ninja turtles and made sure Joseph had his blanket and Michael had his rabbit. I did my best not to douse the boys' excitement despite my fear. I loaded the suitcase and the boys in the car and gripped the steering wheel to maintain control. Between small conversations with the boys I prayed all the way there. "God please help me trust You to take care of them. Please don't let Mark hurt or kidnap them."

We pulled into the truck stop parking lot and parked next to Mark's truck. Mark hurried out of his truck the moment we stopped. He ran to collect the boys in his arms. He followed me to the trunk of my car and put the boys down to retrieve their prized possessions and loaded them in his truck. The boys and he jabbered; I became invisible.

"If I forgot—," I started.

"I'll take care of them," he snapped. "Tell your mom good-bye. We need to go."

The boys gave me a reserved hug and good-bye kiss. A hint of fear and uncertainty shot from their eyes as they turned around. "I love you, boys. I'll see you in a few days. If you need me, just call." Mark shut their doors and drove away. I collapsed into my car. Fear and emptiness gushed from my heart. It took thirty minutes for me to regain control. I drove away, heartbroken, in despair and alone. "God, I'm scared. I have no power or trust in Mark or the court system. Please help me trust You. Guard and protect them and bring them back to me." I sobbed all the way home.

For the next six months the boys were shuttled back and forth between Colorado and Nebraska for one weekend a month. Each time, I experienced the same fear that they weren't safe with Mark and there was nothing I could do to protect them. I also endured harsh words and attitudes from the boys. Their words illustrated that they were mad at me because they believed their dad was all better and somehow I had tricked them. My heart was slipping into a spiral of helplessness.

Summer break came and the court-ordered, eight-week visitation weighed heavily on my heart. I packed the boys and their belongings, then drove to the now familiar truck stop to meet Mark. My thoughts went crazy. Mark could handle them for a weekend and fool them into thinking he was all better. What would he do when the boys fought or messed up because they were children? Would he hurt them, or would he take them and run away to avoid any consequences? It took all my strength to maintain self-control. Eight weeks was forever in my mind. My sense of dread grew. I pulled up and parked next to Mark. My heart ached. We said our good-byes and I collapsed in my car as I watched them drive away. "God, help me," I sobbed. I'm not sure how I made it home, but I did.

Chapter 26

"All I have seen teaches me to trust the creator for all I have not seen."
—Ralph Waldo Emerson

The first few weeks of summer left me in a heartbroken daze. I talked to the boys for a few minutes every Monday night. They never wanted to talk long and I didn't force the issue. At least I knew they were alive, but I was devastated.

I snapped to life when I received a call from Dad telling me that Mom was in the hospital because her kidneys were failing. The doctors told us Mom was not a candidate for a kidney transplant because of the condition of her body. The best they could do for her was to put her on dialysis three times a week. We were all scared and aware that this was the beginning of the end of Mom's life.

Mom spent several more weeks in the hospital so the doctors could stabilize her and insert a blood port access for dialysis in her arm. She took it all in stride on the outside, but she was still terrified she would lose her legs. Mom had less energy and that required using a wheelchair. I spent a week helping Dad rearrange the house to make sure we could get Mom around in her wheelchair.

I was cleaning the living room when a police officer came to the front door. I couldn't imagine why he was there. I opened the door. He asked me my name and said he had been looking for me. He handed me an envelope, said I had been served, and then walked away. Was this one of Mark's thugs after me again? My heart sank as I took the envelope and closed the door. I sat down, opened the envelope, and read the legal-sized paper. Dated July15th, it stated, "You are hereby ordered to appear in court on Tuesday, August 18th to defend the following accusations made against you: Drunken disorderly conduct in front of your sons; beating your oldest son and chasing him out of a two story window; indecent exposure in front of your sons; and deemed unfit to care and provide for your sons. Witnesses for the father: Michael, Joseph, and Dr. Dumo, counselor for the boys."

"Oh, God, what's happening? Help me." I grabbed my purse and headed for Lance's office. I ran in, demanding to see Lance immediately. I paced the foyer until Lance led me to his office. I handed him the papers.

The look on his face said it all. "Darla, Mark's suing you for sole custody."

"How can he do this?" I flung my arms in the air and paced the floor. "These are all lies. What can we do?"

"Mark's brainwashed the boys over the last six months, and especially these last seven weeks. He's manipulated them into testifying for him. He's using them to control, hurt, and damage you so he can have sole custody."

"This isn't right. How can I save my boys?" I walked over to Lance's desk.

Lance held out his hands. "Darla, you can't. Because the boys are listed as witnesses, all you can legally do is put the boys on the stand and let me do my best to get them to tell the truth."

"You mean cross-examine them? I could never do that to them." I cried and buried my face in my hands for a few minutes. "The boys have been Mark's victims all their lives and now you're asking me to let you victimize them, too? If they speak these lies, it will haunt them forever. There has to be another way."

Lance came around his desk and sat in the chair beside me. "Darla, if these charges are all lies, what are you afraid of?"

"I fight my mind every day to stop the tormenting fact that I was a bad mom for not being able to stop their abuse for so many years. Hearing it from myself is bad enough. I don't know where my mind would go if I heard these things from the mouths of my babies. They are the only good that has come out of my life."

"Darla, stop right there." He held my hand. "You did the best you could with the knowledge and resources you had. Against all long-term odds with abuse, you got out and tried to show them a different way. They are stuck in a hard spot. I agree they don't understand the consequences of speaking lies about you, but I'm also not sure they will understand why you would sign them over to Mark. In their eyes it will look like you are giving up on them, even though we both know you never have or will. You have two giants between you and the boys, Mark's anger and the court system. You can choose to fight or you can sign over custody to Mark so they don't have to testify."

I stood up and paced the floor a few more minutes. "Are you telling me I have no other legal recourse than to prove my boys are liars?"

"No, I'm sorry. Not legally." he shook his head.

I held my hand up. "I can't accept this." I grabbed my purse and stormed out. I left the office and stopped at a park to figure another way out. "God, I don't understand. I'm scared and powerless and I don't know what to do. I can't save them anymore, but You can. I have to trust what happens is in Your bigger plan and that You will return my boys to me one day, somehow, someway."

Twenty-nine days dragged by as I searched for any means to change the outcome. I contemplated running away with the boys; maybe we'd be safe on the Indian Reservation. I was sure Mark couldn't come there, but we would be isolated and without support from anyone. What if I forced my boys to repeat Mom's life by moving there? The biggest problem was that they were with Mark. I had no access to them. I waited and prayed, but I was helpless and hopeless once again. I felt utterly defeated.

The dreaded day arrived. I parked at the courthouse and prayed. "God I can't believe the boys are better off with Mark, but I have to trust You. Help me know what to say and do."

I entered the courtroom with my attorney, Lance. Court was called into session and Judge Chapman read the charges. Each attorney pled his side and I was doing my best not to fall apart.

I was sworn in and took the seat at the witness stand. I looked at the boys, but they stared at the floor while Mark sneered. Everything I'd feared about Mark taking the boys was coming true. He manipulated and brainwashed them to come to court and tell lies about me to win his love. Mark hoped their testimony would force me into signing their custody over to him. Legally, I had two options: first, I could put them on the stand and have my attorney victimize them. The thought of Lance breaking them to get to the truth was unbearable. My second option was to stop all this by signing over custody. *God help me. I don't want them to live with the guilt of lying about me on the stand.* I gripped the handles of the chair to maintain control. I asked for the boys to be removed from the courtroom for a statement I wanted placed on record. The judge agreed.

I looked heavenward and took a deep breath. "Judge Chapman, is it true I have no legal way to fight this without the boys taking the stand to testify against me?"

"I'm sorry, no," he replied with a frown.

I took a deep breath and clinched my chair. "I don't believe with the past record of Mark's abuse and what he has done in the past has shown him to be responsible. I do not believe that having the boys testify against any parent is in their best interests." I squeezed my chair to keep control. "These are boys and they love both parents and want to please both parents. Putting them in that situation is not in their best interest. I don't want the kids to suffer anymore or be used as pawns in this proceeding. I don't want them used and manipulated and hurt anymore."[1] I glared at Mark and looked back at the judge.

My voice cracked and I could feel the dam of sorrow fracture under the pressure. "I will not allow my boys' hearts and minds to be attacked and mutilated on the stand. I won't allow more adults to pulverize their value and destroy their hearts. They've been abused and victimized by Mark, but I won't join him. One day they will learn the truth and be set free. For now I have no choice but to keep them from being destroyed. Therefore, I'll sign custody over to Mark."

Mark snickered and grinned. God alone held back the anguish that welled up in the corners of my eyes. I bit my lip while I signed the papers. To prevent my heart from exploding, I walked out of the courtroom; I was shattered to my core. Somehow I found my car and crawled inside as my heart disintegrated.

All the pain, brokenness, and poison from the years of abuse amputated my chance to be a good mother. This was my end. Half my heart was numb from the instant chop. The other half throbbed with phantom pains longing to have the boys again. The blackness of the pit inside was screaming my name. "Darla, you've failed again. You always do. Come down here and stop feeling your pain. Just disappear. No one will notice. What's the use of going on? Your boys are gone and they will hate you."

My mind flashed over the dozens of times I couldn't prevent the boys from being hurt and abused. I should have killed Mark. Every word of Mark's accusations was false, but the final accusation exploded in my head: "I was unfit to care for and provide for my sons." It was true. I was a horrible mother. I didn't and don't deserve to care for my sons. Being a mom was my dream, my purpose, and the reason for my every breath. *I've failed. I'm defeated. I give up. There's no reason to breathe now.*

Blackness overtook my mind until I saw a flicker in the dark. With all the strength I had left, I cried out, "God, how can Mark be the best for the boys? How could he sacrifice them? How? I have failed them, God. I've tried to keep the boys safe and loved and happy, to shield them, to make everything all right. In the end I failed. God, I can't bear this pain, this sacrifice. I want to die."

A loud squawk and a dark shadow startled me. I took a breath and looked up. Two crows stared at me on the hood of my car. I heard God's spirit whisper, "I take care of the birds, I have taken care of you, and I will take care of them. Trust in Me and lean not unto your own understanding. The boys will need you more in the future than in the past. Come to Me and I will give you rest; trust in Me alone." I felt a peace beyond all my understanding abide in me once again. "Become the best person in Me you can be to help them when they came back. Believe and live."

I reached for God's strength and determined I would believe and prepare for the boys' return someday. I couldn't stay absorbed in my pain. I had to prepare myself to be strong for them when they finally came home. I would cling to a new hope and promise God spoke to my heart. That's all I had and I'd hold to it for dear life.

Chapter 27

"This is one of the miracles of love: It gives a power of seeing through its own enchantments and yet not being disenchanted."

—C. S. Lewis

I changed my focus to helping Dad take care of Mom. When my boys entered my mind, I chose to thank God for taking care of them and returning them one day. I sent them cards and letters to let them know how much I loved them. I tried to call them, but there was no answer or response. I hoped and prayed something got through, but I never knew. God helped me understand their silence was not their hearts, but the confusion in their minds. They felt abandoned by me, and they were too young to understand that I did it all for them.

I recalled Erma saying the boys are simply trying to win the love and the approval of their dad. This helped me to avoid falling into a deep pit of despair. Most days it took all my faith and strength not to beat myself up and let my mind disappear into the black abyss. I fought hard to keep my mind from thoughts of ending it all. I would remember how I felt when Mom was mentally checked out and I was choosing to be there for the boys when they came back. I clung to God's promise that one day they would return.

A year passed and Mom's dialysis took its toll on her body. Dad and I were at home having lunch when the dialysis clinic called to tell us we needed to take Mom to the hospital. Her blood entry port in her arm was clogged. Dad and I drove Mom to the hospital immediately and she was admitted.

We visited with Mom for a while. "You know, Darla, I've realized something in the last few years," Mom said.

"What's that, Mom?" I said.

"In the end, the memories you've made with your family and friends and the people who are beside your bed and in your heart are all you have. Promise me you'll make memories with the boys and those you love. Promise me," she pleaded.

"Yes, Mom, I will. Get some rest and we'll be back in a little while." I kissed her and left with Dad. We went to the lounge and rested for a few minutes. A nurse came by and asked Dad to fill out some more forms.

I decided to go back and visit with Mom. I eased the door open. Mom was looking up into the corner of the room. Her mouth moved and she radiated joy from her smile, but I couldn't hear a sound. "God, help me," I prayed as I closed the door and eased quietly to her side.

"Mom, what do you see?" I asked.

"It's beautiful, Baby, the colors, the sights, the sounds." She inhaled. "And the smells. Oh, look at the beautiful mountains and the waterfalls. The grass is a brilliant green and the flowers are magnificent. Smell this flower." She handed me an imaginary flower.

"Who do you see, Mom? Do you see Grandma Dorothy?" I asked.

"Yes, we've been visiting. She's here with Grandma Elaina and the rest. They're dressed in radiant white. They're under the trees," she said.

"How does she look?" I said.

"She's beautiful and she's running all over. Oh, look at that grassy hill over there." She pointed.

"What else do you see?" I asked.

"Don't you see all those picnic tables covered with barbeque ribs? They look delicious." She licked her lips.

"Mom, what—," I started as Mom sat up and turned to me.

"Oh, hi, Baby. When did you come in? I must have dozed off." She smiled and reached out for a hug.

"Just now, Mom." I fought back the tears in my eyes. She saw heaven, and God let me see it through her. Deep in my heart I knew she was going home soon.

"Are you okay?" She noticed the tears in the corners of my eyes.

"Yes, Mom, I'm fine. What did you order for dinner?" I rubbed my eyes as the assistant delivered her dinner tray.

"Roast pork, I think. But I want to eat dinner alone," Mom said.

"I'll stay and keep you company." I volunteered.

"All of you need a break and dinner. Darla, take your dad out and relax for a minute. Go on." She waved at us.

"Are you sure, Dolly?" Dad asked. He had quietly joined us, listening to our conversation.

"Yes, Sam, go." She held her arms out for hugs.

Dad hugged and kissed her good-bye first. I followed and lingered a little longer as if this was my last hug. "Mom, I love you and I'll see you later." I bit my lip to hold back the tears and left the room.

"I love you guys. Have fun," she said.

We went to dinner and I felt a tension building in my heart. We ate for a few minutes. Suddenly, I felt a flutter in my heart and an ache in my soul. I looked down at my watch. It was 7:08 p.m. Mom had flown to heaven. I didn't and couldn't say a word. We finished and started back to the hospital.

"Darla, drop me at the door while you park. I need to stop at the nurses' station again." Dad ambled out and shuffled to the main entrance.

I couldn't find a parking place and had to park far away from the entrance. With each step toward the door, another wave of panic erupted in my chest. I ran up the staircase and down the hall to Mom's room. As I turned the corner, I saw several nurses and doctors rushing into Mom's room. Other nurses cried when they saw me. I dashed to the doorway and stopped. Mom was lying in bed, lifeless. She had a breathing tube sticking out of her mouth. The attention of all the nurses and doctors was on my father, who was lying unconscious on the floor.

"Darla, I'm sorry," Erin said. She was one of the nurses who had taken care of Mom for years. "Your mom's in heaven, but we didn't get things finished before your dad walked in. The doctor thinks he's had a heart attack." She held my hand as a gurney came for Dad.

"Oh. God, help me," I cried. The nurses hoisted him on the gurney, hoses attached to him.

"You'll need to go with your dad to the ER to see what can be done for him." She attached my hand to Dad's gurney, and we all rushed down the hall.

"Dad, I'm right here. Can you hear me?" I asked.

He raised his hand and glanced at me through the oxygen mask. He looked scared and devastated. "Oh, God! Help me. Mom's gone and Dad's had a heart attack. No one's here but you, Lord, once again. Give me strength to know what to do and say," I prayed as I trotted beside the gurney.

They placed us behind a curtain and hooked Dad's hoses to beeping machines. "Dad," I whispered in his ear.

"She's gone," he sputtered through tears.

"Yes, Dad, she's in heaven," I cried.

"Dad, if you want to go and be with her, you can," I gasped, fighting to keep control. "Please don't stay unless God asks you to."

He squeezed my hand and cried for several minutes while he prayed. "Darla."

"Yes, Dad?" I clutched his hand and leaned closer.

"I need to stay a while longer. It's not my time yet." He looked at me, drenched in tears.

"Dad, it's okay either way, but I have to say I am glad you decided to stay." I smiled and hugged him.

The doctors came to take him to x-ray and for other tests. "I'll let the doctors do their thing. I need to make some calls and take care of Mom. Are you okay if I leave?"

"Yes, you need to go take care of Mom," he cried.

"Don't worry, Dad, I'll take care of everything. You concentrate on getting better. I love you." I kissed him and left.

Thank you, God, for letting Dad stay a while longer. One day he'll meet Mom for a picnic in heaven, but he's with us for now. I found my way back to Mom's room. The nurses had taken out the tube and draped a blanket over her. She looked as if she were asleep. Mom was finally free at last. She'd found peace. I walked over to her and clung to her skin suit, which was now cool to my touch. I kissed her cheek. "Good-bye, Mom. I love you." I held her and wept.

I fought to contain my sadness since I had to call everyone to let them know Mom was in heaven. I pulled out my cell phone and dialed Mark. The phone rang and rang.

"Hello," Mark answered.

"Mark, please don't hang up," I pleaded. "I need to let the boys know Grandma D went to heaven. Can I talk to them?"

"They're in bed and have school in the morning. Getting them upset tonight wouldn't be good for them. I'll tell them tomorrow." The receiver clicked silent. I dialed the number again, but Mark didn't answer. Things hadn't changed; Mark was still cutting me off from my sons.

I collapsed in a chair. "God, why can't I have my boys with me?" I was tortured by the separation between us. Nothing made sense. I was overwhelmed by waves of sadness and pain. I buried my face in my hands and sobbed. In the middle of my despair, I felt an arm encircle me. It was Erma. We embraced one another and wept. After regaining our composure, through more waves of tears I told her everything that had happened. Erma comforted me until I was calm. She gave me a bear hug, then walked over and said her good-byes to Mom. She had lost her best friend and I had lost my mom.

Erma helped me call Conner in California. He had moved there fifteen years ago and had made a good life for himself. He was devastated and said he would be on the next plane out. The last call I had to make was to the funeral home.

Over the next two days, I attempted to call Mark ten times. He finally answered my calls and we made arrangements to exchange the boys at the truck stop so they could attend the funeral. I drove alone, bouncing from sadness to a spark of hope that the boys still loved me after being isolated from me for over a year. We pulled in the parking lot at the same time. I stopped and stepped out of the car. The boys ran into my arms and we all sobbed. It felt so good to hold them in my arms, to smell them, to be able to show them my love. Mark was silent and I was grateful.

The boys said their good-byes to Mark after he had loaded their suitcase into the trunk. I hugged and kissed them again before they got into the back seat. They had grown so much. They were now ten and twelve, and I had missed it all. I shut their doors and sat in the front seat waiting for them to buckle their seatbelts.

"Mom, when did Grandma die?" Michael asked.

"May thirteenth, the Thursday before Mother's Day. Why?" I looked at his tear-streaked face in the rearview mirror.

"Dad never told us Grandma died until yesterday. He said he forgot what day she died. I wanted to know the exact day she went to heaven." Michael wiped his tears.

Five days had gone by before Mark told them that Grandma D had died. I bit my lip and stared ahead to keep the volcano of rage capped. He's still the same monster.

"Can we see Grandma?" Joseph asked.

"Yes. We're on our way to the funeral home. Boys, this will be hard. I want you to know her body's present but her spirit's in heaven. It hurts to say good-bye, but we know she's already home. I wiped the tears from my eyes and handed each of the boys a tissue.

"Can I do anything for you two?" I asked.

They shook their heads in silence and stared at the slideshow of cows, windmills, and rolling hills of dead grass flashing past their windows.

The boys' despair stacked onto mine at the sight of Mom's body. My heart and soul wrenched. I helped them say good-bye and Erma took them outside for a break. I stayed inside and walked to Mom's body. "God, I know I'll see Mom again, but I'm heartbroken. We had so little time to share, heal, and love. Take care of her." I looked at her body one last time, thankful that her spirit was gone.

The funeral brought together many old friends, a few family members, and several nurses who had cared for Mom over the last ten years. The nurses' streams of tears and comments revealed Mom's impact on their lives. Mom was right; we are God's light in this dark world and we are often unconscious of where He shines. Mom was gone but we were still alive waiting for the sadness to subside.

The day came to send the boys back to Mark. It was life renewing to have them and earth shattering to let them go. I kept replaying the message of God in my mind all the way to the truck stop and back. He promised to bring them back to me, and I had to trust Him. This was the only way to keep my pain under control.

For several months the boys and I talked every week. Gradually, we talked less and less and I could feel the canyon between our hearts growing deeper and more distant. One evening I asked them what was going on.

"Mom, you're too controlling and a liar and we don't want anything to do with you," Michael yelled. "If you get a lawyer, we'll run away. Leave us alone." Michael slammed the phone down. My heart crumbled. This couldn't be his heart, but I heard his words.

"God, why did you make me a mother to have me lose my sons to their abusive dad over and over again?" I screamed. "I can't take this pain. I just can't do it anymore." I grabbed my purse and car keys and ran through the rain to my car. I drove off in the rain, lost in a flash flood of sadness, guilt, and ultimate condemnation. Snapshots of the torment in my past engulfed my mind and soul. I surveyed the road for answers and spotted a bridge. Maybe everyone would be better off if I drove into this bridge and died. I turned my steering wheel toward the bridge.

A serene voice submerged my spirit. "I know the bigger picture. The boys will return and they will need you in the future to help them heal and understand. Work on yourself and you'll be ready for their return."

I pulled the car over and stopped, right in front of the bridge, and wept. "God, ease the ache of my empty arms. I resolve to believe You will return my boys back into my arms. Without hope I have nothing. I surrender all my anxieties and their lives to You, Lord."

The temptation to fall into depression and self-loathing grabbed at my heart. I decided to stop and visit Erma. Maybe she could help me find some relief from my torment. She was sitting at the kitchen table with a fresh cup of coffee.

"It looks like you need a hug." Erma held out her arms. I fell into them and cried.

"I don't believe the boys don't want me. I know it was Mark's words I heard, not Michael's. I have to do something."

"What are your options?" She helped me to a seat and went to pour another cup of coffee. She placed it in front of me as she sat beside me.

"I could go to court once again and fight for custody. Now that they're older, they can choose." I stopped and looked down. "I'm asking them to choose, just like Mark did. I can't do that unless the boys come to me and ask me for help."

"I believe you're right. If you wait for them to come to you, it will be by their free choice, not manipulation." She smiled and pointed skyward. "God's always at work even when we can't see any results. Keep believing and trusting in the Creator of the universe. He will get you through." Erma and I prayed and talked about life some more. I left with God's unexplainable peace.

Chapter 28

"The best and most beautiful things in the world cannot be
seen or even touched. They must be felt with the heart."
—Helen Keller

Six long, silent years passed with no contact from the boys. I
decided I would go to Michael's high school graduation uninvited. I
wanted him to know I was proud of him, even if he never spoke to me
again. I walked in to meet the glares and whispers of Mark and his
new wife. After the ceremony Michael came to me and let me hug him
and tell him I loved him. Joseph said hi, but he kept his distance. The
canyon between our hearts and the anger in their eyes sliced open all
the scars of failing as a mom. They were right to be angry. Life had
dealt them a bad hand. My anguish left me breathless, and I did my
best to go on with my life.

When Mom died I moved in with Dad to take care of him,
harboring a secret hope that we could find the same healing Mom and
I had found. He was sad, and he welcomed my love for a while. Over
several months, though, Dad's words revealed his heart hadn't
changed where I was concerned. For some reason, deep inside he was
angry with me. I went with him to doctor appointments and helped
him every week with what I could, even though he always found
something wrong with me or my actions. I honored him with my care,
but I kept a wall around my heart as I made a life for myself.

Eventually I married a kind and loving man named David. Our
hearts were focused on God and we laughed and enjoyed our life.

David and I were kindred spirits and it was easy to be myself with him. I didn't have to walk around on eggshells or worry that he would hurt me. I got a taste of what God had in mind when both individuals care for the other in a healthy way. I was also blessed to have his parents, Buddy and Karen, in my life. From the first time we met we had a heart and spirit connection. They had grown close to my heart and they moved from Kansas to live next door to us. At last I had a healthy, happy family and love around me consistently.

David and I took many real estate investing classes over a year, and we ended up in Texas rehabbing and flipping several properties. We would work for a while in Texas, then we would come back home to Colorado to rest.

I took God's leading and worked on my heart, beliefs, and mind-set during those years. God brought healing, peace, and assurance that He was in control. I focused on the love and wonderful support I had at home.

I kept an eye online for the graduation ceremony for Joseph because I hadn't received an invitation or announcement from him. David and I attended uninvited, and we came face to face with a wall of anger from both boys. They told me they would be moving around, and if they wanted to talk to me, they would call. They turned around and walked away.

My heart shattered. David did his best to console me, but this wound was too deep. I closed myself off for days to everyone but God. "God, I know I caused their anger. Help me know what to do." A picture of Dena popped into my head. I took a chance Dena would be working and drove to her office. The years had been good to her; she gave me a bear hug and led me to her office.

"Darla, you look great. What in the world brings you here?" She smiled at me.

I burst into tears and took a seat. Dena sat next to me and held my hand. "Dena, my life's great, except for the boys." I wiped my tears. "I fought so hard to get them out of the abuse, and in the end they've ended up living with Mark for years. He prevented any contact with me and now I fear I've lost them for good. My husband and I just returned from Joseph's graduation. We went uninvited and experienced the familiar hate and anger from Mark and the boys." Tears streamed down my cheeks. "I did my best to change their lives." I pressed my hands to my chest and opened them to Dena. "Dena, I've failed them. I can't blame them for hating me."

"Darla, take a deep breath." Dena inhaled deeply several times, waiting for me to join her. "Fill me in on your life so I know how to help you."

I told her about signing custody over to Mark and, in between tears, related all the other heartaches that followed. She listened quietly and held my hand.

"There's no simple answer when it comes to understanding the complexities of people and abuse," Dena said. "However, there are patterns and experiences I have seen that can help you. To understand their anger you'll need to look at things from a young child's perspective and their longing to be loved."

Dena's words scratched a lesion, reminding me of my pain as a little girl. The boys must feel just like I did when my parents sent me away, abandoned and unloved. I'd failed to protect their hearts from the same pain and scars. "Dena, I made my choices because I didn't see I had another way to protect the boys." I blurted out to ease my guilt and shame.

Dena squeezed my hand and leaned closer. "I'm not beating you up and I don't want you to beat yourself up when I talk about these abuse dynamics. We're looking back to find the answers that will move you forward through your pain. You didn't know any other way to handle it and survive until you gained more knowledge and chose to change your life. There's no way to climb a set of stairs all at once. So let's take this a step at a time, okay?"

"Okay, I'm ready." I sat up.

"For many years the boys have been isolated from you and exposed to Mark's hate and anger for you, demonstrated in his words and rage," Dena said. "I would surmise from past case experience, they went along with it in hopes Mark would give them the love and attention they craved. When a developing child is subjected to hate and anger for years, the lines of reality, truth, and lies become fuzzy. In a sense they are brainwashed into believing another person's ideals and pains." She held my hand and I sighed. "The first step is to see their view of Mark. They saw his weakness and brokenness and heard the reason for his horrible behavior was their fault or yours. It was never safe to be angry with him or at him. The second step is to see how they saw you. You appeared strong and in control of yourself, their caretaker, able to fix things, and pretending all was well. They saw your strength and never saw you as a victim, because you hid Mark's abuse to you."

"If they didn't see me as a victim and I was strong, they probably wondered why I didn't fix everything." I wiped my tears. "And if I could fix everything, why did I let them go? They heard me promise I'd protect them, but I broke it."

"As children and victims, they had no power, control, or understanding of what was going on," Dena said. "They copied you by trying harder to please Mark in hopes of receiving love."

By this time my heart was scalding from the pain. I sobbed tears of guilt and shame.

"Darla, in a child's mind, when you say you're sorry, it's because you did something wrong. Abused children have a hard time separating empathy from guilt with the word sorry." Dena squeezed my hand.

"So what you're saying is, in their eyes when I told them I was sorry, I was admitting their pain was my fault?"

Dena nodded in agreement. "Your apology gave them the opportunity to fall into the pattern of blame they learned from Mark to help them cope with their pain." Dena patted my hand. "You also took the fall for their anger because you felt guilty and responsible for their pain as a mother, even though you didn't cause their abuse. All of their pain, confusion, and uncertainty collided with their child reasoning and understanding to create their anger."

"No matter what I did they would be angry." I sighed. "The stronger I was, the angrier they got. There was no way for me to win this battle. Now what can I do?" Hopelessness fell on me and I buried my face in my hands. "I've ruined their lives."

"Darla, stop right there." Dena shook me and I looked up. "The responsibility for the abuse is Mark's. He hurt them. He refused to change. He's the one who has brainwashed them. Divorce is devastating to children, but when you throw in abuse, it's debilitating. I know this is painful for you, but we need to put the responsibility for the abuse on Mark where it belongs and keep the focus on the boys to help you get through this."

"I understand." I sat up and composed myself. "I want to know how to help them and myself. Please continue."

"Even though you left the abuse, the boys' core desire for their dad to love them never left. Once they returned to Mark and realized he was the same and they believed that you couldn't or wouldn't rescue them anymore, they were angry all over again," Dena said. "From their conversation with you at the graduation, they show me that they are still stuck in their child thoughts, understanding, and emotions of the abuse cycle. Until they choose to look at the truth about you and Mark as adults and are willing to understand these dynamics and allow themselves to heal and forgive you and Mark, they will be angry with you. Their minds must look at true facts to make sense of their pain. Until they do, they will blame someone. The safe one is you."

Dena looked into my eyes. "Darla, be gentle with yourself. You did the best you could with the skills and resources you had at each stage of your life. You've grown into a strong, confident, and healthy woman because you got out. You can't fix your boys, only yourself."

Dena was right; I had grown and I could only change me. My heart still hurt, but I found a new clarity and understanding that helped me see and be at peace with where the boys were emotionally. I also realized they had their own road of healing to travel, something only they could do.

"Darla, keep your heart open and gentle with safe healthy boundaries so the boys know they will always be welcome to come home. Encourage them and speak to them without judgment or condemnation."

"I will. Thank you for everything." I hugged Dena and headed home.

I left her office with a new understanding. "Lord, let me pass the mercy and grace you have given me to the boys. Thank you for this revelation."

My evening devotion revealed how Jesus always kept his arms and heart open to Peter no matter what he did or didn't do. Jesus loved him where he was and encouraged him along the way. There was no judgment or condemnation, only love, forgiveness, and grace. This devotion confirmed I had the right plan to love my boys. God brought healing, peace, and assurance He was in control.

Chapter 29

"Miracles happen to those who believe in them."
—Bernard Berenson

David and I were exhausted from working on our real estate investments for the past year. We came home for a rest and we wanted to spend more time with Buddy and Karen. Our time away had left our house in need of some repairs. All four of us worked in the yard all day and then decided to go out for dinner.

At the restaurant we laughed about the day and relaxed. Suddenly, Karen grabbed my arm. "I think Joseph just went out the door."

I sprang up and dashed out the door calling, "Joseph! Joseph?" I noticed he was with a young woman; they whirled around.

"Mom?" Joseph looked shocked.

An enormous smile burst forth, revealing my joy as I noticed the young woman was pregnant. The corners of their mouths turned slightly upward.

"Joseph, it's great to see you." I smiled. "Are you living in Fort Collins?"

"Yes, Mom, we are." Joseph grabbed the young girl's hand. "This is my girlfriend, Rachael."

"Hi, I'm Darla." I held my hand out to her.

"Hi, I'm Rachael." She shook my hand. "Glad to meet you."

Joseph glanced around, avoiding direct eye contact. "Joseph, it seems I will soon be a grandma. What a wonderful surprise!" I smiled and continued, "I know a lot has happened in the past and I'm sorry. If

210

you can find it in your heart to forgive me, I would be grateful and honored to have the opportunity to be a part of all of your lives."

"Mom, let's take this one step at a time." Joseph pulled back to create space while Rachael smiled from ear to ear.

"Please think about it. Can I give you my phone number?" I asked.

"Sure." Joseph handed me his phone.

I punched my number in and handed it back to him. "If you would like to come to dinner one evening, we would love to have you," I said. "Just give me a call." We said our good-byes and I watched them walk away.

My heart leapt with hope. Joseph moved to where I was. He couldn't hate me. "God, please let him call." I went back to the table and told my family the great news.

A few days later Joseph called and arranged to come over Friday evening with Rachael. I was elated.

Friday came and David and I cooked dinner with his parents, hoping and praying they would come. They arrived right on time and we strived to love them and not question them.

Gazing at my family around the table my eyes pooled with tears. "Mom, are you okay?" Joseph questioned while gently touching my hand.

With tears rolling down my cheeks I replied, "My cup runneth over with joy and thankfulness. God brought you back, plus two. I am truly blessed." God kept his promise.

*   *   *

Joseph and Rachael spent more time with us and our hearts were slowly healing. It was an honor to see our first grandchild growing in Rachael's tummy. They were very young and afraid, but we let them know in our words and deeds we were there for them. Rachael had two months until her due date when our real estate business required us to go back to Texas for at least six months. My heart was torn. Joseph and I were slowly making progress, and the thought of going away was too much to bear. We talked about our dilemma as a family and Joseph and Rachael decided to come to Texas once the baby was born to help us with our investment properties. We were ecstatic; I could leave for Texas knowing they were close behind us.

David and I went back to Texas and concentrated on our business and on our relationship with God. We grew closer to God through the teachings of Pastor Tom at church and in our Sunday school class. Our small group helped us grow through books and studies about the kingdom of God, who we were in Christ, the power of the name of Jesus, the gifts and talents God had given us, and the purposes of our life's journey. One night in a dream I saw myself being thrown into a fiery furnace and Jesus walking around with me, just like in the story of Shadrach, Meshach, and Abednego. I came out unharmed. I heard God calling me to share my life with other women to inspire, encourage, and bring them hope and evidence of His grace and mercy. I didn't know how, but I determined to believe and follow the path as He directed me. God had redeemed my life, and I would serve Him no matter what happened.

In spite of the miles, Rachael and I grew close, but Joseph still barricaded his heart from mine. I thanked God for bringing him back into my life and I kept praying one day God would help him take the rest of his walls down.

One evening in October the phone rang; Joseph and Rachael were on their way to the hospital. David and I drove seven hours to the hospital to see our first grandson. We arrived one hour before he made his entrance into this world. Once I held Noah in my arms and I hugged Joseph, I saw the wall between us begin to crumble. Noah was born on October 13th. This was the same date Mom had died in 2000 and the day David and I had met in 2001.

Michael came to see Noah and I was reunited briefly with both of my boys once again. "God, thank you for being my redeemer. You took Mom and gave me David, Buddy, Karen, Michael, Joseph, Rachael, and now Noah as my family." On the drive back to Texas, David and I decided to change our plans. Being grandparents changed everything. We would complete our business in Texas and return home to Colorado permanently.

Chapter 30

"There are two kinds of people: those who say to God,
'Thy will be done,' and those to whom God says,
'All right, then, have it your way.'"
—C. S. Lewis

We set out to find a property manager to handle our properties and tie up all our loose business ends so we could go home. We stayed involved in church and our small group. It was going to be sad to say good-bye, but I was ready to go home.

My friend, Robin, asked me to go with her to a retreat called The Road to Emmaus. The minute she asked me, my heart jumped and I agreed. I didn't know what to expect, only that I needed to go.

Robin picked me up on Friday evening. We drove to the retreat out in the country; there were many buildings and a sanctuary. We settled into our rooms before the opening session of the retreat. Everyone met in the sanctuary and waited for the pastor's welcome.

"You have all come to this retreat on God's purpose." Pastor Jim held out his hands to us. "Jesus knew you before you were ever in your mother's womb. He created you, He chose you, and He gave His life for you. Many of you here need to hear and believe that God truly loves all the good, the bad, and the ugliest parts of you, unconditionally, no matter how you feel. I encourage you to open your hearts, ears, and eyes and give God the opportunity to love and heal your heart while you are here in this safe haven." He prayed over us and asked us all to sit in silence and share our hearts with God before he dismissed us in prayer.

My heart stirred. "God, I've come to know You and I believe You made me and chose me. I'm so grateful that You died for my sins and You love me. Lord, please reveal what's constantly trying to pull me down. Help me see what You see in me." After the service we had refreshments and played a game, then went to bed. I knew I was in the right place.

After breakfast, we gathered in a meeting room to hear our first speaker, Hillary. She shared her battle of feeling less than everyone else. The way she saw herself and devalued herself kept her trapped in paralyzing guilt and shame.

Hillary explained that guilt is rooted in our actions or non-actions. Shame is rooted in the very flesh essence of who we are. She said the change in her life occurred when she realized the difference between healthy and unhealthy guilt and shame. The healthy guilt and shame are moral alarms from God. They are meant to lead us to ask Jesus for forgiveness when we sin. Without forgiveness from Jesus, she was pummeled with her unhealthy thoughts and beliefs that she wasn't valuable enough to receive any good in her life except by chance. Receiving and living in God's forgiveness freed her from her unhealthy thoughts and eventually her self-degrading habits.

The barbs of bad shame and guilt tumbled over in my mind while Hillary finished her story. I was trying to make sense of her statements. From my first breath, Satan used every chance to tell me I wasn't worthy of the air I breathed. It was reinforced by the words and actions of Mom and Dad and then by my rape and abusive marriage. *But, God, you brought Erma to love me and teach me more about You.*

You have helped me see that You care about every hair on my head. You have been faithful even when I tried to fix Mark, my boys, and myself on my own. Forgive me for my independence. You have never left me and You have always taken care of me. I can't imagine my life without You. I don't want to feel anymore bad guilt and shame. Lord, give me a revelation. Please set me free. The applause of the crowd for Hillary brought me back to reality.

We all took a short break and then gathered into small groups of eight with a leader for each group. Beth, a kind, soft-spoken woman, led our group. She instructed us to go outside and find a quiet place where we could talk to God. In this place she wanted us to ask God to reveal the largest wounds in our hearts and write them down in our journals. She didn't know what she was asking me to do, and I wasn't sure I wanted to go there again.

I went to a wooden bench next to a flower garden and opened my journal. A geyser of pain shot to the surface of my heart when I wrote about my introduction by Mom, Dad's reaction to my rape, and my abusive marriage. All the healings of the whys and hows about domestic violence only scratched away the base of my mountain of bad guilt and shame. I couldn't feel anything but the hot coals of terror and devastation my boys had endured burning through my heart and soul.

"God, I've asked for Your forgiveness and theirs, but I still feel like a failure as a mother and a person. Please forgive me. I can't change the past. My heart breaks at the distance between my sons' hearts and mine. Help them to understand and see how much I love them. Help them to forgive me so they can be free. Help me see what

I'm missing so I can be free from this torment." I pulled my knees to my chest and sobbed.

Beth saw my pain and sat down beside me, waiting for me to regain my composure. "Darla, I see the agony in your heart. I don't have the answers you need, but God does. Can I pray with you?"

"Please." I sighed.

"Lord, we come to you, our Maker, Savior, and Redeemer. Darla's hurting from some horrendous wounds in her past. We ask You to reveal the answers she needs to be able to trust You. I pray that You engulf her being with Your grace and love until she surrenders all her heart and receives all that You have prepared her for. Heal her heart today." Beth hugged me.

"Thank you," I whispered.

"It's time for the next speaker. Are you ready to go in?"

"Yes." I took a deep breath, walked into the meeting room, and took my seat.

The next speaker, Jill, was waiting at the podium. She shared her struggle to find peace with herself from her bad choices that brought pain to her loved ones for many years. Her words of living in an abusive marriage skewered my heart. I was looking in a mirror once again. I glanced at the floor to fight back the tears.

Jill's revelation came from understanding the difference between God's forgiveness and the mystery of His grace. "Forgiveness is relational," Jill paused. "We ask God for forgiveness. We ask forgiveness from another person and we give it to another person. God forgives us and we are called to forgive one another, but scripture never says anything about forgiving ourselves. Even though we constantly hear it from society, professionals, and even other believers, it isn't in scripture." She held out her bible. "Because I bought into this concept, I kept trying to find a way to pay for all the bad I had done or change the bad person I thought I was. I was trying to do what only Jesus could do on the cross: save me, forgive me, and pardon me. Only Jesus, without sin, could ever pay the ultimate price to give us forgiveness. I realized I had to receive and accept it in my heart, spirit, and soul through God's grace, which I don't deserve and I can never earn. I came to a place where I chose to walk in the gift of God's grace and completely let go of my shame. He took my shame away. It was my choice to keep remembering it but if God forgives us, who are we to dredge it all up over and over again?" Jill paused.

My mind was spinning. *Jesus, You've paid the price. I kept thinking and trying to make up for the past pain. Forgive me for not understanding and living in Your grace and forgiveness. There's nothing I can do or could have ever done to earn these gifts. Lord, give me a revelation to understand the mystery of Your grace.* I closed my eyes and felt the weight of my past lift from my heart. I felt like I could float away.

Jill's voice brought me back to earth. "I pray that all of you find this same place of grace. Thank you." We all clapped and were dismissed for dinner.

I learned so much that day. I felt a freedom I had only dreamed about. My heart was healing and I was grateful for this retreat.

After dinner we gathered again in the meeting room. We sang a song of love to Jesus and lined up to go out the south door. We stepped outside into the crisp night air. The stars were glorious and ever so near. We walked along the sidewalk and I saw yard signs with the names of the other women at the retreat. I looked for my name along the path and began to wonder if I'd missed it or if they overlooked me. Suddenly, there it was at the entrance of the building. I mattered. I belonged.

I crossed the outer threshold into the dark sanctuary. My heart erupted in awe and my knees wobbled. My eyes beheld a sanctuary filled with friends from my church holding candles, echoing our song. A tsunami of God's love wrapped in His discernible grace submerged my essence, leaving me breathless. A bright light suddenly revealed angels singing, and a man dressed in brilliant white picked me up and held me in His arms. A picture of my boys at birth flashed in my mind, bringing waves of the unconditional love I felt for them. This ushered tidal waves of unconditional love I now felt coming from Jesus, washing over me.

"Darla, feel and accept how much I love all of you. Embrace and walk in My grace. You alone were worth every lashing, every tear, and every drop of blood I shed. My daughter, trust in Me completely and believe you alone were worth dying for." My spirit drank in every word from Jesus.

I placed my hand in His and surrendered my heart to His grace. In seconds I felt the fragmented pieces of my life pull together with the ointment of God's grace. All the scars and painful memories became vibrant pigments and brushstrokes in the masterpiece of art God was creating me to be. I finally believed I was worthy of His unconditional love, and I choose to live in it every day. His love clothed in grace has set me free.

Last Thoughts

My story is evidence that in Christ my past didn't chain me to the same painful future. Even though bad things happened, God's love and grace changed the effects they had on my heart and life. God took my shattered heart and created a beautiful mosaic masterpiece I can share with others who believe they are unlovable or unloved, and who are tormented with unhealthy guilt and shame.

We are all at different places in our spiritual walk and understanding of God and ourselves. I pray that you become hungry for a personal relationship with God. His grace is real and when you seek Him, you will find He loves you just as you are, where you are, and who you are. He is the only answer I can provide to heal you from the wreckage of your life. Only He can redeem your life and set you on a new course, stronger and full of peace. Seek Him with your whole heart. He's waiting with open arms. You will find His forgiveness and love, and like me, you can learn to walk in the miracle of His grace.

About the Author

Meet Darla Colinet

Darla Colinet honestly shares her heartache and triumph in her first memoir, *Under the Staircase: Hearing God's Voice in the Darkness*. As a teacher of various women's Bible studies and through the Women's Ministries at Timberline Church, she actively encourages and inspires women with God's truths. She has a heart for helping all domestic violence victims through local and national organizations. She lives in Fort Collins, Colorado, where she continues to write as well as speak and teach. Be empowered to live an authentic and abundant life by reading Darla's blog and books, or by hearing her passion for life at one of her speaking engagements and you will discover, as she has, that God's not done with any of us yet!

Acknowledgments

Through Christ I can do all things. This book would not be possible without Him. He gets my first thanks.

This memoir is the story of my life, but it took the help of many friends, family, and professionals to create it. I can't thank them enough for their encouragement, faith, prayers, and pushing me on when it was a struggle. With their love, support, and prayers I finished.

My heart was honored to have my angel mom, Louise Breyer, help me work through the most difficult memories and keep a loving heart.

I'm thankful for Kerrie Flanagan, my chief editor and now a good friend. She guided me through my story and helped me find my unique voice and style.

The following people were very supportive and helped me polish the final draft. Thanks to Jenny Breyer, Theresa Cook, Bette Albrecht, Pat Marotta, Beth Allen, and Karen Dumler.

My final manuscript would not have come together without the professional touches from Jennifer Top, my copy editor. The cover was a combined effort of Jennifer Top and myself.

There are no words to express my gratitude for my two sons who love their imperfect mom and share their lives with me.

Thank you to all my extended family for your encouragement and prayers.

NOTE: Chapter 26, note 1. Quote from original court transcript

Resources

National Domestic Violence Hotline: 800-799-SAFE (7233) or 800-787-3224 (TTY)

Books that have helped me:

When Helping You Is Hurting Me: Escaping the Messiah Trap by Carmen Renee Berry

Beauty for Ashes by Joyce Meyer

Facing Your Giants: The God Who Made a Miracle Out of David Stands Ready to Make One Out of You by Max Lucado

The Power of Your Words: How God Can Bless Your Life Through the Words You Speak by Robert Morris

Boundaries: When to Say YES, When to Say NO, to Take Control of Your Life by Henry Cloud and John Townsend

The DNA of Relationships (Smalley Franchise Products) by Gary Smalley, Greg Smalley, Michael Smalley, and Robert S. Paul

NIV Study Bible

Message Bible

www.ingramcontent.com/pod-product-compliance
Lightning Source LLC
LaVergne TN
LVHW051506080426
835509LV00017B/1934